This publication is a precious jewel, both adding to the unli
presence as Srimad-Bhagavatam and reflecting that splendour.
both the text and its graphic presentation, enabling a full and p
the Bhagavatam's structure and profundity.

- HH Devamrita Swami

I am sincerely grateful to the Bhaktivedanta Vidyapitha for their dedicated efforts to present this publication – Bhagavata Subodhini. I pray that each reader may enter deeper and deeper into the knowledge and devotional love (Bhakti Ras) of the essence of all Vedas – Srimad Bhagavatam.

- HH Radhanath Swami

Bhagavata Subodhini is a praiseworthy project for deepening our appreciation of the Bhagavatam, particularly from the insight of Srila Visvanatha Cakravarti. By concisely organizing his analysis of the work, the devotee will be able to relish both the Bhagavatam and Visvanatha's realizations. Caitanya Mahaprabhu has accepted Bhagavatam as the main pramana since it is the conclusion of all scriptures. By understanding its import the devotee will be able to grasp the theology, practice and goal of the Vedic tradition in a most compact form.

- HH Bhanu Swami

pibata bhāgavatam rasamālayam. Bhagavata Subodhini is an excellent study guide that makes Srimad Bhagavatam more relishable and easier to digest. Drawing strength from the Bhaktivedanta Purports and Bhagavad commentaries by Srila Visvanatha Cakravarti Thakura, Bhagavata Subodhini is a great tool for an in-depth, systematic and scrutinising study of Srimad Bhagavatam. I strongly recommend this masterpiece for one and all, young and old, alike. My hearty congratulations to the Bhaktivedanta Vidyapitha team of Govardhan Eco-village for this invaluable publication. I pray that they do not stop till the goal of publishing guides for all the twelve cantos is reached.

- HH Lokanatha Swami

Srila Prabhupada has left for us a treasure house of literature, which is the essence of the Vedas. To unpack it more into details of what is being said and the congruency of how that knowledge is being presented is nicely done in this Bhagavata Subodhini. It is a very noble attempt. I find the Subodhini series a great aid in making our presentation more complete and interesting – both for the students and the teachers and for general audience who are interested in going deeper into the philosophy and practice of Krishna Consciousness. Subodhini will help people get attracted to study Srila Prabhupada's works, and in a more easily understandable way. It is a great project, and we commend the devotees who are doing such hard work.

- HH Chandramauli Swami

Given the importance of the Bhagavata Purana and the increase in general interest in its content, study guides such as the present publication are to be enthusiastically welcomed by students of the text. The initial two volumes of Bhagavata-Subodhini, comprising the first three skandhas of the Bhagavata, offer a chapter-by-chapter analysis, with a more detailed focus on the most significant verses. Such volumes will be most useful for classes and workshops.

- Prof. Paul Sherbow, Rutgers University

I found Bhagavata Subodhini very interesting and useful, for it presents the contents of Bhagavatam in a systematic and lucid manner. I am very happy that the devotees in our society are producing such wonderful literature based on Srila Prabhupada's books and commentaries of other acharyas. I like the fact that in one book I have access to commentaries of different acaryas, that too presented in an interesting tabular format which made it easy and clear to read. This book is like a Bhagavatam digest. It helps the preachers in their presentations on Bhagavatam. I wish I had access to such books before. I encourage devotees to come together, for this kind of study and contemplation on the Bhagavatam.

- HH Bhakti Purushottama Swami

It is a guide, I use to get a bird's eye view of a Chapter, to spot out Diamond like sections for deeper contemplation and nectar like slokas for relishing and repeating to others. It has increased my appetite for Bhāgavatam study and gain great spiritual advantage. Thanks to Bhaktivedanta Vidyapitha for their dedicated efforts in making Srila Prabhupada's master piece work more easy and accessible for all. Hare Krishna.

- HG Radheshyam Das

The challenge for teachers in today's distracting world is to catch and retain students' attention. Students, even if they can avoid distractions, still can easily be overawed by the vastness and seeming complexity of shastra. In such a setting, the Subodhini series comes to the aid of shastra teachers and shastra students by presenting the foremost texts of our tradition accessibly and appealingly. As our movement strives to create more resources for promoting education, the Subodhini series prepared by Gauranga Darshan Prabhu counts among the most valuable resources available for devotees in their efforts to savor and share the treasure of shastra that Srila Prabhupada has gifted us.

- HG Chaitanya Charan Das

BHĀGAVATA SUBODHINĪ

Enriching the Experience of Śrīmad-Bhāgavatam study

CANTO 7

BHAKTIVEDANTA VIDYAPITHA RESEARCH CENTER
TRUTH · TRADITION · TRANSFORMATION

GAURANGA DARSHAN DAS

Bhaktivedanta Vidyapitha Research Center
ISKCON Govardhan Eco Village, Galtare, Hamrapur (P.O),
Wada (Taluka), Palghar (District),
Maharashtra, India - 421303
www.vidyapitha.in | Email: info@vidyapitha.in

Published and Printed by:

Tulsi Books (A division of Sri Tulsi Trust)
7. K. M. Munshi marg, Girgaum Chowpatty, Mumbai – 400007
www.tulsibooks.com | Email: tulsibookssales@gmail.com

BHĀGAVATA SUBODHINĪ CANTO 7
ISBN: 978-93-81283-64-6
First Printing – April 2019: 2000 Copies

Dedicated to

HIS DIVINE GRACE
A.C. BHAKTIVEDANTA SWAMI PRABHUPĀDA

Founder-*Ācārya* of the International Society for Krishna Consciousness

yair īdṛśī bhagavato gatir ātma-vāda
ekāntato nigamibhiḥ pratipāditā naḥ
tuṣyantv adabhra-karuṇāḥ sva-kṛtena nityaṁ
ko nāma tat pratikaroti vinoda-pātram

How can such persons, who have rendered unlimited service by explaining the path of self-realization in relation to the Supreme Personality of Godhead, and whose explanations are given for our enlightenment with complete conviction and Vedic evidence, be repaid except by folded palms containing water for their satisfaction? Such great personalities can be satisfied only by their own activities, which are distributed amongst human society out of their unlimited mercy.

[*Śrīmad-Bhāgavatam* 4.22.47]

ACKNOWLEDGEMENTS

Words fall short in expressing my gratitude to Śrīla Prabhupāda who presented the *Śrīmad-Bhāgavatam* with his lucid explanations in a language understood by the modern world. I am indebted to Śrīla Viśvanātha Cakravarti Ṭhākura for his *Sārārtha-darśinī* commentary that further helped me understand the contents and flow of the *Bhāgavatam*. My sincere thanks to His Holiness Bhanu Swami Maharaja for presenting it in English. *Bhāgavata Subodhinī* is nothing but a concise representation of the *Bhāgavatam* based on the explanations of these great *ācāryas*.

I express my earnest gratitude to my beloved *guru* His Holiness Radhanath Swami Maharaja for enlightening me on the ideal mood of scriptural study and encouraging me with his kind blessings. I also thank him for envisioning the Govardhan Ecovillage project that offers a perfect ambience and facility for śāstric study.

I am forever indebted to Gauranga Prabhu, my guide and source of inspiration in all my humble endeavors. It is his ardent desire to see the scriptures being systematically studied by the devotees, and it is my fortune to be of some assistance to him.

I am grateful to Sakha Gadadhar Prabhu for drawing all the illustrations of Nṛsiṁha-deva and Prahlāda in this book. I thank Vikas Prabhu, Vijay Krishna Kumar Prabhu and Uddhava Priya Prabhu for their kind assistance in compiling the Appendices.

My sincere thanks to Dr. Shrilekha Hada for her wonderful inputs in improvising the manuscript. Special thanks to Vrindavan Priya Prabhu for providing the image of his Śrī Śrī Lakṣmī-Nṛsiṁha Deity for the cover page.

I am thankful to the Tulsi books team for publishing the book. Special thanks to dear friend Raas Gopal Prabhu for his printing coordination and assistance.

It is not possible to name all my friends at Govardhan Ecovillage whose warmth and support inspire me in all my services.

– Gauranga Darshan Das

CONTENTS

Thematic Compilations

Appendix

Introduction

In the rainy season, muddy paths in villages are often not used, and thus they get covered with grass. Similarly, when authentic scriptures are not studied for long, pure knowledge becomes covered by speculative and unwanted theories that misdirect the human society.

Scriptures present pristine wisdom descending directly from the Supreme Lord, showing us the path of transcending miseries and going back to Godhead. When thick grass covers a pathway, it is difficult to walk on that path or sometimes the path is not even recognized. Similarly, if one generation chooses not to study, understand, apply and spread the knowledge of the scriptures, the later generations would have no precedence and inspiration to study or follow them, or even become aware of them.

Therefore, it becomes the responsibility of sincere spiritual seekers to read and assimilate the scriptural principles and guide the future generations. This *Bhāgavata Subodhinī* is a humble attempt to facilitate and simplify the study of our most vital scripture, *Śrīmad-Bhāgavatam,* by giving its structure, flow and gist in a concise form.

The *Śrīmad-Bhāgavatam* is the ripened fruit of the desire tree of the Vedic scriptures. This transcendental literature is nondifferent from Lord Kṛṣṇa, who has returned in the form of this book (*śrī-kṛṣṇa parivartitā*) to shed light on the misdirected civilization of Kali-yuga. It was compiled by the literary incarnation of Godhead, Śrīla Vyāsadeva in the maturity of his knowledge. The study of *Bhāgavatam*, done in line with the explanations of bona fide *ācāryas* in the Vaiṣṇava *paramparā*, gives the sincere reader an unparalleled understanding of the Absolute Truth, which is not possible by one's own speculative efforts. In fact it is Lord Kṛṣṇa Himself who speaks through the disciplic succession to enlighten the serious students of the *Bhāgavatam.*

The glories of *Śrīmad-Bhāgavatam* are limitless. It presents the rarest knowledge about the identity, nature and character of the Supreme Personality of Godhead Śrī Kṛṣṇa and His various incarnations, and also His wonderful devotees.

The *Śrīmad-Bhāgavatam* has Twelve Cantos that represent the limbs of Lord Kṛṣṇa's transcendental body.

pādau yadīyau prathama-dvitīyau tṛtīya-tūryau kathitau yad-ūrū
nābhis tathā pañcama eva ṣaṣtho bhujāntaraṁ dor-yugalaṁ tathānyau
kaṇṭhas tu rājan navamo yadīyo mukhāravindaṁ daśamaḥ praphullam
ekādaśo yasya lalāṭa-paṭṭaṁ śiro'pi tu dvādaśa eva bhāti
tam ādidevaṁ karuṇā-nidhānaṁ tamāla-varṇaṁ suhitāvatāram
apāra-saṁsāra-samudra-setuṁ bhajāmahe bhāgavata-svarūpam

"The First and Second Cantos of the *Bhāgavatam* are Śrī Kṛṣṇa's lotus feet. The Third and Fourth Cantos are His thighs. The Fifth Canto is His navel. The Sixth Canto is His chest. The Seventh and Eighth Cantos are His arms. The Ninth Canto is His throat. The Tenth Canto is His beautiful lotus-face. The Eleventh Canto is His forehead. The Twelfth Canto is His head. I bow down to that Lord, the ocean of mercy whose colour is like that of a *tamāla* tree and who appears in this world for the welfare of all. I worship Him as the bridge for crossing the unfathomable ocean of material existence. The *Bhāgavatam* has appeared as His very Self." *[Padma Purāṇa]*

The expanse and depth of the *Bhāgavatam* is better appreciated from the commentaries of great *ācāryas*, or spiritual teachers. Śrīla Prabhupāda mentions in his purport to the first verse of *Bhāgavatam*: "...there is no doubt about the authority of the *Bhāgavatam*. Within the past five hundred years, many erudite scholars and *ācāryas* like Jīva Gosvāmī, Sanātana Gosvāmī, Viśvanātha Cakravartī, Vallabhācārya, and many other distinguished scholars even after the time of Lord Caitanya made elaborate commentaries on the *Bhāgavatam*. And the serious student would do well to attempt to go through them to better relish the transcendental messages."

Śrīla Prabhupāda compared *Bhāgavatam* study with taking *darśana* of the deity of Lord Kṛṣṇa, which is done gradually from His lotus feet to the lotus face. He emphasizes a step-by-step study of the *Bhāgavatam* in his preface to *Bhāgavatam*: "The only qualification one needs to study this great book of transcendental knowledge is to proceed step by step cautiously and not jump forward haphazardly as with an ordinary book. It should be gone through chapter by chapter, one after another."

While reading this expansive scripture of eighteen thousand verses, the readers might sometimes find themselves lost in the multitudes of conversations, keeping track of various personalities and episodes, or understanding the technical sections. Therefore, sometimes the readers tend to read selective sections or pastimes from the *Bhāgavatam* rather than reading chapter by chapter.

In the *Bhāgavata Subodhinī*, I have made a humble attempt to present the flow of the *Bhāgavatam* concisely, based on the commentaries of Śrīla Prabhupāda and Śrīla Viśvanātha Cakravarti Ṭhākura. This book aims at presenting the structure of the *Bhāgavatam* chapters and connections between different verses and sections, with simplified flow charts and tables. This book is not meant to be a replacement for a detailed study of the *Bhāgavatam* itself, but a complement for devotees, students and curious readers. I hope that this bird's eyeview of the *Bhāgavatam* helps the readers in their deeper study of the book to fully delight in its splendour.

Features of Bhāgavata Subodhinī

- *Canto at a glance:* Overview of the entire Canto, presented in a flowchart.
- *Chapter overview chart:* Provides a bird's eye view of the major sections and subsections of a chapter in a block diagram.
- *Section:* A group of verses that fall under the same heading.
- *Subsection:* A sub-group of verses within a section.
- *Verse synopsis:* A brief summary of a verse highlighting its import as explained by the *ācāryas*. All the verses are duly numbered and some keywords of the Sanskrit verse are given in brackets.
- *Verse:* A most vital Sanskrit verse of the chapter, which is worth memorizing, presented in the flow, sometimes with its line-by-line meaning in a tabular form.
- *Table:* A list of items under a section.
- *Flow chart:* Gives a bird's eye view of the sequence of stages in a process.
- *Link:* The connection between two verses, sections, subsections or chapters
- *Note:* A vital comment or a brief explanation on a verse or section, mainly related to the flow of the chapter, for enhancing the understanding.
- *Footnote:* Deeper insights, additional information and application perspectives.

All the links, notes and footnotes are based on the commentaries of Śrīla Prabhupāda and Śrīla Viśvanātha Cakravarti Ṭhākura.

Special verses section contains selected verses from the *Bhāgavatam* Canto that carry a deep significance in terms of philosophy (*siddhānta*) and emotion (*bhāva*). Citations of different angles of understanding these verses as given by the *ācāryas* are listed.

Thematic compilations section presents lists of verses on various prominent themes of the *Bhāgavatam* Cantos, duly categorized. The objective of this section is to make the reader appreciate the cross-sectional prominence of a specific theme revealed in various chapters.

Appendix presents extensive lists of reference material from the *Bhāgavatam*. Unlike thematic compilations, they are more direct in nature with little or no analysis, such as, names of the Supreme Lord, character portrayals and analogies.

Nomenclature: To keep the reading of *Bhāgavata Subodhinī* relatively simple, the referencing for verses is done in a standard format. The following abbreviations represent their equivalent expanded forms given against them:

- SB – *Śrīmad-Bhāgavatam*
- BG – *Bhagavad-gīta*
- CC – *Śrī Caitanya-caritāmṛta*
- 7.2.6 – SB Canto Seven, Chapter Two, Verse Six
- 7.2.6 P – Śrīla Prabhupāda's purport on 7.2.6
- 7.2.6 V – Śrīla Viśvanātha Cakravartī Ṭhākūra's commentary on 7.2.6

References to other books are explicitly stated.

With all the above features, the *Bhāgavata Subodhinī* aims to enrich the experience of your *Śrīmad-Bhāgavatam* study. I sincerely hope and pray that this book is of some assistance in the study and revision of the sincere readers of the *Bhāgavatam*, translated and commented by Śrīla Prabhupāda and the other *ācāryas*. I seek forgiveness for any unintended discrepancies in this work and would like to be informed of any improvements required. I invite you to dwell on the glorious teachings of *Śrīmad-Bhāgavatam* and experience its enlivening effect.

Bhāgavata Subodhinī simplifies the apparent complexity in understanding the Bhāgavatam, by uncovering and integrating the explanations of Śrīla Prabhupāda and the previous ācāryas, thus catering for the taste and needs of avid readers, scholars and even newcomers to Śrīmad-Bhāgavatam.

The Flow of the Seventh Canto

Note: This section gives a very brief outline of the first six cantos of the *Bhāgavatam* and a more detailed overview of the Seventh Canto. For the detailed overviews of the first six cantos, please refer to the previous four volumes of *Bhāgavata Subodhinī*.

Srimad-Bhāgavatam is the ripened fruit of the tree of Vedic wisdom compiled by Śrīla Vyāsadeva at the maturity of his knowledge. It is the *granthāvatāra* of Lord Śrī Kṛṣṇa, narrating the pastimes of His various *avatāras*. Glorified as a *mahā-purāṇa*, it contains ten subjects namely: (1) *Sarga:* universal creation by the Supreme Lord, (2) *Visarga:* secondary creation by Lord Brahmā, (3) *sthānaṁ:* planetary systems, (4) *poṣaṇam:* protection by the Lord, (5) *ūti:* impetus, (6) *manvantara:* the reign of Manus, (7) *īśānukatha:* the topics of God and His devotees, (8) *nirodha:* annihilation, (9) *mukti:* liberation, and (10) *āśraya:* the supreme shelter, Lord Kṛṣṇa. The ultimate purpose of the first nine topics is to glorify the tenth topic, *āśraya-tattva*. Although all these topics are spread in all the cantos of the *Bhāgavatam*, they are more vividly described in the specific cantos.

The First and the Second Cantos of the *Bhāgavatam* are considered the Supreme Lord's lotus feet and they form a perfect prelude to the rest of the *Bhāgavatam* by introducing the reader to its key philosophical concepts and prominent characters. These cantos also establish *bhakti-yoga* as the topmost spiritual path and Lord Kṛṣṇa as the Supreme Personality of Godhead. Wonderful prayers by devotees like Kunti and Bhīṣma, and Lord Kṛṣṇa's reciprocation with them, the birth of Parīkṣit Mahārāja and his activities, and the history of *Bhāgavatam* are presented. Further, there are descriptions of the process of creation, *virāṭ-rūpa*, *catuḥ-ślokī Bhāgavatam* and finally the definitions of the ten topics of the *Bhāgavatam*.

The Third and the Fourth Cantos correspond to the Supreme Lord's thighs and predominantly describe the topics of *sarga* and *visarga,* through the conversation of Vidura and Maitreya. The Third Canto also describes time, embryology, family life, Sāṅkhya, *bhakti-yoga*, *aṣṭāṅga-yoga*, *jñāna-yoga*, *karma*, the spiritual and the material worlds. We further read the pastimes of Lord Varāha, the description of

Vaikuṇṭhaloka, the household life of Kardama Muni and Devahūti, and the teachings of Lord Kapila in the Third Canto. The Fourth Canto is very rich in its content. It unveils the stories of admired personalities like Lord Śiva, Sunīti, Dhruva, Nārada, Aṅga, Pṛthu and the Pracetās, who all showed extraordinary examples of *bhakti*. One can also learn about the unfavourable attitudes in *bhakti* from the mistakes of characters like Dakṣa, Suruci, Vena, Indra and Prācīnabarhi. The positive transformation undergone by many of these personalities, mainly due the intervention of devotees, adds to the glory of *bhakti*. Furthermore, the prayers of pure devotees like Dhruva, Pṛthu and the Pracetās disclose the foremost aspiration of a devotee – to hear *kṛṣṇa-kathā* in the association of devotees.

The Fifth Canto corresponds to the lotus navel of the Supreme Lord. In this canto, Śukadeva Gosvāmī continues the topic of *visarga* and describes the dynasty of Priyavrata, the other son of Manu. Priyavrata's dynasty consists of several notable personalities like Āgnīdhra, Nābhi, Lord Ṛṣabhadeva and Bharata in his three lives as a King, a deer and a *brāhmaṇa*.[1] All these episodes culminate in the glory of *bhakti*. The latter half of this canto discusses *sthānam*, the positioning of various planetary systems within the structure of the universe for the inhabitation of various living entities. The canto concludes with a description of various hellish planets.

The Sixth Canto of the *Bhāgavatam* corresponds to the chest of the Supreme Lord. It is majorly centered on the theme of *poṣaṇam*, or protection offered by the Supreme Lord to His devotees, although they sometimes transgress the laws of *dharma*. This canto begins with the glorification of the Lord's holy names through the episode of Ajāmila. Later Śukadeva Gosvāmī resumes the topic of *visarga* and describes the living entities generated through the sixty daughters of Dakṣa. As a part of that, the offenses and the struggles of Indra are described along with the glories of a pure devotee Vṛtrāsura. Vṛtrāsura's previous life as King Citraketu reveals the insubstantial nature of material relationships, compassion of a devotee in uplifting a struggling soul, the need to be careful in dealing with other devotees, and the eagerness of the Supreme Lord to reclaim His devotee. The canto concludes with the transformation of Diti and Indra by devotional service.

Thus the first six cantos of the *Bhāgavatam* describe the glories of the Supreme Lord and His devotees and predominantly describe *sarga, visarga, sthānam* and *poṣaṇam*.

---

[1] In the Third, Fourth and Fifth Cantos, Maitreya describes the family lines of Svāyambhuva Manu's descendants: Devahūti (3.21-4.1), Ākūti (4.1), Prasūti (4.1-7), Uttānapāda (4.8-4.31) and Priyavrata (5.1-15).

Ūti – The inclination to act

The Seventh Canto and the Eighth Canto of the *Bhāgavatam* represent the arms of the Supreme Lord. The Seventh Canto describes *ūti* or inclination, which is of two types – auspicious and inauspicious. The auspicious and inauspicious inclinations of the *jīvas* lead them to perform pious and impious acts, which becomes the cause of their future happiness and distress in various births. The inauspicious inclinations of Hiraṇyakaśipu were caused by the anger of the four Kumāras (who cursed Jaya and Vijaya to go to the material world). The auspicious inclination for pure *bhakti* of Prahlāda arose from the mercy of Nārada Muni (who enlightened Prahlāda when he was in his mother's womb).

The Seventh Canto describes two types of *bhakti*: (*i*) *śuddha-bhakti* or pure devotional service of Prahlāda described in the first ten chapters, and (*ii*) *miśra-bhakti* or mixed devotional service of persons following *varṇāśrama* described in the last five chapters. In *miśra-bhakti, bhakti* is mixed with *karma* or *jñāna* as a major or minor element.

God's apparent partiality

At the end of the Sixth Canto, Śukadeva Gosvāmī described that Diti lamented for the death of her sons Hiraṇyākṣa and Hiraṇyakaśipu, who were killed by Lord Viṣṇu in the form of Varāhadeva and Nṛsiṁhadeva, being instigated by Indra (SB 6.18.23). Referring to this, Parīkṣit Mahārāja asked Śukadeva Gosvāmī about the apparent partiality of Lord Viṣṇu in favouring the demigods and killing the demons. Śukadeva Gosvāmī replied that the demigods flourish when *sattva-guṇa* is prominent and the demons flourish when *rajo-* and *tamo- guṇas* are prominent, due to the influence of time. But the Supreme Lord is neutral, impartial and equal to everyone. He is especially inclined to His devotees in reciprocation to their devotion. However, even when He punishes and kills the demons, He only benefits them by giving them liberation. Thus the Lord's mercy and His punishment are ultimately meant to uplift everyone. (7.1)

God's astonishing mercy

In this connection, Śukadeva Gosvāmī refers to a conversation between Nārada Muni and King Yudhiṣṭira that took place at the Rājasūya sacrifice (the entire Seventh Canto is based on this conversation). At that time, Lord Kṛṣṇa beheaded Śiśupāla and thus liberated him. Wondering at this, Yudhiṣṭira asked Nārada how could Śiśupāla who was always envious and offensive towards Kṛṣṇa attain liberation. Nārada explained that when one's envy or anger towards Kṛṣṇa leads to a deep absorption in Him, one attains Kṛṣṇa. Then he related how the doorkeepers of Vaikuṇṭha, Jaya and Vijaya, were cursed by the Kumāras, and took three births in this world as: Hiraṇyākṣa and Hiraṇyakaśipu, Rāvaṇa and Kumbhakarṇa, Śiśupāla and Dantavakra. (7.1)

Lamentation and pacification

Hiraṇyakaśipu, the king of the demons, was grief-stricken when his brother Hiraṇyākṣa was killed by Lord Varāha. He intended to kill Lord Viṣṇu and instructed his demoniac associates to persecute innocent people, stop all religious activities and the worship of Viṣṇu. He performed the last rites of Hiraṇyākṣa and pacified his relatives by saying that the material body is perishable and the spirit soul is eternal. Even demons speak philosophy, but they don't intend to act on it. Hiraṇyakaśipu narrated the story of king Suyajña who died in a battle. Suyajña's wives lamented and didn't allow the dead body to be burnt. At that time Yamarāja came as a small boy and enlightened them by narrating the story of Kuliṅga birds. (7.2)

An intelligent attempt to avoid death!

Desiring to become immortal, Hiraṇyakaśipu later performed severe austerities to please Lord Brahmā. The effect of his austerities tormented the demigods, who then reported to Brahmā about Hiraṇyakaśipu's intentions to occupy Brahmā's position, and appealed him to take suitable action. Obliged, Brahmā went to Hiraṇyakaśipu who became emaciated by penance. Brahmā appreciated his determination, revived him and asked what he wanted. Hiraṇyakaśipu praised Brahmā in various ways and begged that he may not meet death – from any living entity created by him, inside or outside a house, during day or night, on the ground or in the sky, by any weapon, human, animal, demigod, snakes and so on. However intelligent one may be to avoid death, he can't be smarter than the Supreme Lord. (7.3)

A classic example of misusing power

Lord Brahmā granted the rare benedictions asked by Hiraṇyakaśipu. Demons control their senses with great determination to receive boons, but by the power of those very boons, they become victims of their uncontrolled senses. Envious Hiraṇyakaśipu conquered all directions, oppressed the demigods, usurped sacrificial shares, controlled the nature, made everyone forcefully worship him and always remained intoxicated internally and externally. The demigods approached Lord Viṣṇu for protection and the Lord reassured them that Hiraṇyakaśipu would be vanquished when he teases his noble son Prahlāda, endowed will all transcendental qualities. (7.4)

The faith and wisdom of a young devotee

Little Prahlāda was sent for education to the school of Śaṇḍa and Amarka, the sons of Śukrācārya. Prahlāda didn't like the political philosophy taught by his teachers. Once Hiraṇyakaśipu affectionately asked Prahlāda to speak on what he considered the best of all subjects. Prahlāda replied that for an attached householder, giving up family life and taking shelter of Lord Hari is the best. Hiraṇyakaśipu laughed at it and told Prahlāda's teachers to protect him from the Vaiṣṇavas who might go to *guru-kula* in disguise. Śaṇḍa and Amarka took Prahlāda back to *guru-kula*, chastised him and forcefully taught him *dharma, artha* and *kāma,* and brought him to his father again. Hiraṇyakaśipu asked Prahlāda to repeat what he had learnt from his *guru*. Prahlāda described the nine processes of *bhakti*. Hiraṇyakaśipu became furious and asked the boy who taught him that knowledge. Prahlāda described the nature and destination of attached householders, and the power of serving a Vaiṣṇava. Enraged, Hiraṇyakaśipu ordered his servants to kill Prahlāda. But all the attempts to kill Prahlāda failed. It was Lord Viṣṇu's responsibility to protect His faithful devotee in all calamities. Finally Prahlāda was sent to school again at the advice of Śaṇḍa and Amarka. (7.5)

Divine teachings in a demons' arena

At *guru-kula,* when Prahlāda's classmates called him to play in the absence of their teachers, Prahlāda spoke to them in sweet words about the futility of material life. One shouldn't waste the valuable human life for sense gratification to get entangled in materialistic family affairs. A human being should perfect one's life by worshiping the infallible Supreme Lord Nārāyaṇa with *bhakti*. Nothing is unobtainable when the Lord is satisfied. (7.6)

The ceaseless flow of bhakti

Prahlāda's friends asked him how he was so enlightened. Prahlāda narrated that when his father Hiraṇyakaśipu went to do austerities, the demigods attacked the demons and arrested his mother Kayādhu. Then Nārada Muni arrived and stopped them saying that the child in her womb was a great devotee. So the demigods offered respects to her and departed. Merciful Nārada Muni brought Kayādhu to his *āśrama* and spoke to her and the child in her womb on great transcendental topics. But she forgot them, and Prahlāda remembered them. Even a child in the mother's womb can know about *bhakti* by the power of a pure Vaiṣṇava. (7.7)

Prahlāda continued to teach his classmates. He described to them the qualities of the eternal spirit soul and that pure soul gets entangled due to material intelligence. *Bhakti* is the best path that disentangles the *jīva* from this material existence. It begins with service to a bona fide *guru,* frees one from lust, greed, illusion and so on, and brings one to the platform of loving devotion unto Lord Vāsudeva. It is in one's best interest to stop struggling for material pleasures, and take to devotional service of Lord Viṣṇu. Thus Prahlāda urged his classmates to take to *Viṣṇu-bhakti*. (7.7)

The final confrontation

Prahlāda's schoolmates loved his teachings on *bhakti* and rejected the instructions of Śaṇḍa and Amarka, who then reported about this to Hiraṇyakaśipu. Hiraṇyakaśipu rebuked Prahlāda and asked him by whose power was he so fearless. Prahlāda said that Viṣṇu is the source of everyone's strength including Hiraṇyakśipu's. Prahlāda advised his father to give up his demoniac mentality and relinquish the real enemies seated within his own heart like lust, pride and so on. Hiraṇyakśipu threatened to kill Prahlāda and challenged him if his God were present in a pillar. Convinced about the all-pervading nature of the Supreme Lord, Prahlāda said, "Yes!" (7.8)

The most spectacular darśana ever

Hiraṇyakaśipu struck the pillar in rage. To prove the words of His devotee(s) true, the Supreme Lord appeared from the pillar in an unprecedented form as Nṛsiṁha-deva, half-man and half-lion. After enjoying fighting pastimes for some time, Lord Nṛsiṁha placed Hiraṇyakaśipu on his lap and killed him at the time of sunset, on the doorway, merely with His nails, thus not violating any of the benedictions of Brahmā. The demigods celebrated the Lord's victory and offered Him various prayers. (7.8)

The prayers that pacified God

Lord Nṛsiṁha-deva who sat on Hiraṇyakaśipu's throne, was not pacified with the prayers of the demiogds. Even Lakṣmī-devī was fearful of approaching Him. Then Lord Brahmā requested Prahlāda to pacify Nṛsiṁha-deva. Prahlāda fell at the feet of the Lord, who then affectionately placed His lotus hand on the boy's head. Prahlāda offered heartfelt prayers that showed his deep humility, devotion, eagerness for shelter, fear of conditioned life, compassion for the fallen souls and his knowledge of the Godhead's unlimited opulence and glories. In his various prayers, Prahlāda indirectly indicated and directly declared that *bhakti* is the ultimate refuge, and that the material opulences are futile. Lord Nṛsiṁhadeva became very much pleased and told Prahlāda to ask for any benediction he wanted. (7.9)

Unmotivated servant and Merciful master

Prahlāda told Nṛsiṁha-deva not to tempt him with boons, and that he wasn't a merchant to trade his devotional service for some material benefit. But if at all the Lord wanted to give him some benediction, he desired not to have any material desires. Yet Lord Nṛsiṁha-deva told Prahlāda to enjoy as the king of demons till the end of the *manvantara*. Prahlāda then requested the Lord to excuse his father, and the Lord said that Hiraṇyakaśipu has been purified along with twenty-one forefathers. Later Lord Nṛsiṁha-deva told Brahmā not to give such benedictions to demons again. (7.10)

Nārada Muni thus concluded his narration about the *mahā-bhāgavata* devotee Prahlāda Mahārāja and the Supreme Lord Nṛsiṁhadeva. Even Brahmā and Śiva cannot understand and describe the Supreme Lord's glories. Nārada then described how Śiva derived his power from Lord Kṛṣṇa to kill the demon Tripura. (7.10)

The four varṇas (social classes)

Yudhiṣṭira Mahārāja then asked Nārada Muni to describe two more topics: *Sanātana-dharma* and *varṇāśrama-dharma*. Nārada Muni first explained that *sanātana-dharma* or the eternal religion of every living entity is to satisfy Lord Hari by performing *bhakti*. He then described thirty qualifications like humility, mercy and nonviolence, by which one can satisfy the Lord. Nārada Muni then described the occupational duties and characteristics of the four *varṇas* namely *brāhmaṇas, kṣatriyas, vaiśyas* and *śūdras*. He also described the duties of a chaste wife and mixed classes. (7.11)

The four āśramas (spiritual classes)

A *brahmacārī* student should live in *guru-kula* and serve the *guru* with submissiveness and sense control, and shouldn't associate with women. (7.12)

A *vānaprastha* should live a simple life in the forest eating only fruits, and give up his life by merging his gross and subtle bodies with the respective material elements. (7.12)

A *sannyāsī* should be detached, independent, peaceful and fully surrendered to Lord Nārāyaṇa. Nārada Muni further described the conduct of a *sannyāsī* by quoting a conversation between Prahlāda Mahārāja and an *avadhūta brāhmaṇa,* who described the futility of material happiness and the joy of renunciation. (7.13)

A *gṛhastha* should offer the results of one's work to Kṛṣṇa and be detached, devoted, neutral, simple, responsible, and maintain others as well. They should follow suitable time and place to perform all religious activities, and worship the deities, *brāhmaṇas* and Lord Acyuta. One should offer charity to qualified *brāhmaṇas* and give up violence towards other living entities. One should avoid the five types of irreligion and cultivate satisfaction. By surrendering to a bona fide *guru*, and following the prescribed methods, one can overcome all *anarthas*. Householders get liberated by giving up family life at the right time, practicing *yoga* and thus perfecting the human life. (7.14-15)

Nārada Muni then describes the body-chariot metaphor, and the paths of *pravṛtti* and *nivṛtti*, gives a summary and concludes with a description of his previous life as a Gandharva named Upabarhaṇa. Finally he glorifies the pure devotion of the Pāṇḍavas. (7.15)

SEVENTH CANTO AT A GLANCE

Part A1

Pure Bhakti

The story of Prahlāda Mahārāja and Lord Nṛsimha-deva

(7.1-10)

Part A1 Pure Bhakti (7.1-10)	Kṛṣṇa's apparent partiality towards demigods (7.1.1-12)	The Lord is transcendental and impartial. Demigods and demons are favored by the prominence of modes, which are instigated by time.
	Kṛṣṇa's astonishing mercy in liberating envious Śisupāla (7.1.13-48)	If somehow one gets absorbed in Kṛṣṇa, even with envy, he attains Him. Śiśupāla and Dantavakra were formerly Jaya and Vijaya cursed by the Kumāras to take three births in this world.
	Hiraṇyakaśipu's austerities and atrocities (7.2-4)	When Varāha killed Hiraṇyākṣa, angry Hiraṇyakaśipu destroys brahminical culture, consoles his relatives and performs austerities to become immortal. Receiving Brahmā's boons, he terrorizes the universe. Demigods approach Lord Viṣṇu, who then reassures them.
	Prahlāda's devotion and Hiraṇyakaśipu's anger (7.5)	Śaṇḍa and Amarka try to teach Prahlāda politics. Hiraṇyakaśipu tests Prahlāda's knowledge and finds out his devotion to Viṣṇu. Later He attempts to kill the Prahlāda, but fails. He sends Prahlāda back to school.
	Prahlāda's teachings to his schoolmates (7.6-7)	Prahlāda describes the futility of material life, teaches bhakti to his schoolmates, and narrates how Nārada Muni enlightened him when he was in mother's womb.

Part A2
Pure Bhakti
The story of Prahlāda Mahārāja and Lord Nṛsimha-deva
(7.1-10)

- Lord Nṛsiṁha-deva's appearance (7.8)
  - Hiraṇyakaśipu rebukes, challenges and threatens Prahlāda. To prove His devotee's words true, the Lord appears as Nṛsiṁha-deva from a pillar and kills Hiraṇyakaśipu. The demigods offer prayers.
- Prahlāda's prayers and Nṛsiṁha-deva's reciprocation (7.9-10)
  - When the demigods and even Lakṣmī were afraid to approach the Lord, Prahlāda pacifies Him with his devotional prayers. Prahlāda doesn't accept any material boons but seeks the Lord's mercy for his father. The Lord departs and Prahlāda is coronated.

Part B
Mixed Bhakti
Varṇāśrama-dharma (7.11-15)

- Sanatana dharma: Eternal occupation (7.11.1-12)
  - 30 qualities by which one can satisfy the Supreme Lord (7.11)
- The Four Varṇas: Social classes (7.11.13-35)
  - The symptoms and duties of four Varṇas, duties of chaste wife, duties of mixed classes. (7.11)
- The Four Āśramas: Spiritual classes (7.12-15)
  - Duties of Brahmacārīs and Vānaprasthas (7.12)
  - Duties of Sannyāsīs and example of Avadhūta brāhamaṇa (7.13)
  - Duties of Gṛhasthas – Time and place for performing Vedic rituals and Deity worship. (7.14-15)

7.1 The Supreme Lord Is Equal to Everyone

- **1-3:** Parīkṣit inquires about the Lord's apparent partiality
  - Lord Viṣṇu is pure, equal, dear and friendly to everyone. So, how does He kill the demons and favor the demigods?
- **4-12:** Śukadeva Gosvāmī gives a philosophical answer
  - 4-5: This is a wonderful question about bhagavān, bhāgavata and bhakti
  - 6-12: Lord Viṣṇu is the controller of the three modes. People flourish according to the prominences of modes, under the influence of time. But the Lord is not partial.
- **13-21:** Yudhiṣṭhira asks Nārada about the Lord's mercy on demons
  - 13-15: At the rājasūya sacrifice of Yudhiṣṭira, Lord Kṛṣṇa beheaded envious Śiśupāla who then merged into the Lord's body.
  - 16-21: Yudhiṣṭhira asked Nārada Muni how could the envious Śiśupāla be liberated.
- **23-33:** Nārada Muni describes the glory of absorption in Kṛṣṇa
  - 23-25: Material body is meant to experience dualities, and one who identifies with the body suffers. But the Lord has no material body so He is unaffected.
  - 26-32: If one's thinking of Kṛṣṇa even with enmity or anger, leads to deep absorption in Kṛṣṇa, one becomes liberated.
  - 33: Śiśupāla and Dantavakra were Jaya and Vijaya in Vaikuṇṭha.
- **34-48:** Nārada narrates the curse and three births of Jaya and Vijaya
  - 34-35: Yudhiṣṭira asked Nārada how could the associates of Viṣṇu fall to the material world?
  - 36-47: Nārada Muni narrated how Jaya and Vijaya were cursed by the Kumāras. In their three births, they became Hiraṇyakaśipu and Hiraṇyākṣa, Rāvaṇa and Kumbhakarṇa, and Śiṣupāla and Dantavakra.
  - 48: Yudhiṣṭira asked about the cause of enmity between Hiraṇyakaśipu and his son Prahlāda.

Link from Canto 6 to Canto 7: In 6.18.23, it was mentioned that Diti burned with anger and lamentation when her two sons Hiraṇyākṣa and Hiraṇyakaśipu were killed by Lord Viṣṇu, being instigated by Indra. This apparently indicates that the Supreme Lord is partial to the demigods and inimical towards the demons. Parīkṣit Mahārāja, as if not tolerating the partiality of Viṣṇu in favoring Indra, inquired from Śukadeva Gosvāmī about this. Actually Parīkṣit understands the truth, but he desired to relish the nectar of the conclusion from the mouth of Śukadeva Gosvāmī. Therefore he asks this question in 7.1.1-3.

1-3: Mahārāja Parīkṣit Inquires About the Lord's Apparent Partiality

1. Equal, yet partial!? – The Supreme Lord (*bhagavān*) Viṣṇu is equal (*samaḥ*), dear (*priyaḥ*) and a friend (*suhṛd*) to everyone. How then did He kill the demons to favour Indra, as if He were partial (*viṣamo yathā*)?

Here Parīkṣit asks Śukadeva, "If the Lord is equal (*sama*), how can he show partiality to the demigods? If he is affectionate (*priya*) and friend (*suhṛt*) to all beings, why is He not affectionate and friendly to the demons?"

2. Why can't the Lord be partial?

He has a form of pure bliss (niḥśreyasātmanaḥ) →	So, He has nothing to gain (arthaḥ) from siding the demigods
He has no material qualities (aguṇasya) →	So, he cannot have fear (udvega) or envy (vidveṣa) of the demons

The Lord doesn't derive happiness from demigods or distress from demons. So, why should He be paritial?

3. Kindly dispel my great doubt (*saṁśayaḥ*) about the qualities (favouritism and ill-will) of Lord Nārāyaṇa (*nārāyaṇa-guṇān*) with positive evidence, O greatly fortunate sage (*sumahā-bhāga*).

Now Śukadeva Gosvāmī glorifies the wonderful question of Parīkṣit Mahārāja and answers it philosophically.

4-12: Śukadeva Gosvāmī Gives A Philosophical Answer

4-5. Question about bhagavān, bhāgavata and bhakti	
sādhu pṛṣṭaṁ mahārāja	O great king, this is an excellent inquiry, because –
hareś caritam adbhutam	(*i*) It is about he wonderful activities of Lord Hari
yad bhāgavata-māhātmyaṁ	(*ii*) It reveals the glories of the devotees (Prahlāda)
bhagavad-bhakti-vardhanam	(*iii*) It increases devotion to the Supreme Lord

gīyate paramaṁ puṇyam	It is sung by the foremost and pious
ṛṣibhir nāradādibhiḥ	sages headed by Nārada Muni.
natvā kṛṣṇāya munaye	Offering obeisances to sage Kṛṣṇa Dvaipāyana Vyāsa,
kathayiṣye hareḥ kathām	I shall narrate the topics of Lord Hari.

6. The Supreme Lord (bhagavān) Viṣṇu is – without material qualities (*nirguṇa*), unborn (*aja*), unmanifest (*avyakta*) and transcendental to material nature (*prakṛteḥ paraḥ*). Yet, by His own spiritual potency, He enters into matter and appears to act like a human being and cause cause subordination or prominence of a *guna*.

7. The three guṇas (modes), *sattva* (goodness), *rajas* (passion) and *tamas* (ignorance)

- belong to *prakṛti*, material nature or this material world
- do not influence the Supreme Lord
- do not increase or decrease simultaneously

The material nature and the modes are under the control of the Lord. He is not influenced by the modes as described in the above two verses, so He cannot be partial.

The inequality of the Lord *seen* everywhere is based on the inequality of the *guṇas*, according to their increase or diminution. The various modes do not work all at once. One mode becomes more prominent by oppressing the other modes, and becomes less prominent by being oppressed by the other modes.

8. Prominence of the modes: Different people flourish in different modes, favoured by the Lord who fosters results according to particular time (*kālānuguṇo*).

- When *sattva-guṇa* is prominent, the demigods and sages flourish
- When *rajo-guṇa* is prominent, the demons flourish
- When *tamo-guṇa* is prominent, the Yakṣas and Rākṣasas flourish

The cause of the increase of a *guṇa* is time. Since the *guṇas* themselves are insentient, they cannot increase or decrease by themselves. The Lord must enter as their controller.

9. The Lord favors different jīvas residing in them like fire in wood, water in cup and ether in pot. An expert thinker can perceive how much the Lord favors a person by seeing his actions.

Timely favouring is not favoritism: With the increase or decrease of a *guṇa*, the people influenced by that *guṇa* flourish or don't flourish. Fire is latent in wood. When there is more wood there is more fire and when there is less wood there is less fire. One does not call this inequality. Similarly, when there is more *sattva*, demigods flourish. At that time, as *rajas* decreases the demons do not flourish. From the common viewpoint this may seem like favoritism but it is not, for when *sattva* is not prominent, the demigods do not flourish.

10. When the Lord desires to create bodies for different *jīvas*, He revives the three modes. As the Supersoul, He enters each body, and conducts creation using *rajo-guṇa*, maintenance using *sattva-guṇa* and annihilation using *tamo-guṇa*.

11. The Lord creates time factor to control the creation but He is not under time. The material energy (*prakṛti*) and the *jīva* act within the limits of time.

12. When time enhances sattva-guṇa, induced by the Lord, the Lord favors the demigods (*sura-priya*), who are in *sattva*, and destroys the demons inimical to them, who are covered by *rajas* and *tamas*. But the Lord's activities are not partial.

The Lord is equal to all, but is specially inclined to the devotees, in the sense that He is reciprocal to their devotion (as Kṛṣṇa in *Bhagavad-gīta: ye yathā mām prapadyante...*). Though this is favoritism to the demigods (*sura-priya*), it is not the Lord's fault, but His ornament.

To elaborate this subject of the Lord's imaprtial nature, Śukadeva Gosvāmī now quotes a conversation that happenned between Yudhiṣṭira Mahārāja and Nārada Muni. This conversation that begins from the next verse continues upto the end of the seventh canto.

13-21: Yudhiṣṭhira Asks Nārada About the Lord's Mercy on Demons

13-15. Formerly, at the rājasūya sacrifice of Yudhiṣṭhira Mahārāja, Śiśupāla merged into the body of the Supreme Lord Kṛṣṇa (*sāyujya-mukti*). Struck with wonder, Yudhiṣṭhira inquired about this from Nārada Muni, in the presence of many sages. Nārada then cited a historical incident.

16-21: Yudhiṣṭhira Mahārāja's questions to Nārada Muni

16. Śiśupāla was envious. This is astonishing that he attained Vāsudeva (*sāyujya-mukti*), which is impossible even for great transcendentalists.

17. Formerly King Vena fell to hell through the *brāhmaṇas* for blaspheming the Lord (*bhagavan nindayā*).

18. Sinful Śiśupāla began blaspheming Kṛṣṇa from his childhood, when he could not even speak properly, even until now. His brother Dantavakra was also similarly evil-minded (*durmatiḥ*).

19. Śiśupāla and Dantavakra, although repeatedly blasphemed Lord Kṛṣṇa, the indestructible Supreme Brahman, their tongues were not attacked by white leprosy nor did they enter the darkest region of hell. This is surprising.

20. How was it possible for such blasphemous and envious people to enter into the body of Kṛṣṇa so easily in front of everyone, which is very difficult?

Śiśupāla and Dantavakra were formerly Jaya and Vijaya, the doorkeepers of Vaikuṇṭha. *Sāyujya-mukti* or merging into the body of Kṛṣṇa was not their final destination, but only a temporary state. They later attained the liberations of *sārūpya* (having the same form as the Lord) and *sālokya* (living in the same planet as the Lord).

Dantavakra's liberation was not yet heard by Yudhiṣṭhira. Nārada would describe it to him later. But Yudhiṣṭhira understood that Dantavakra would die and thus said this.

21. My intelligence is disturbed, by this most wonderful matter, like a flame in the wind. O omniscient sage, kindly explain the reason for this.

22. Nārada was pleased to hear Yudhiṣṭhira's request. Nārada Muni knew everything and thus began to reply in front of everyone in the sacrifice as follows.

23-33: Nārada Muni Describes the Glory of Absorption in Kṛṣṇa

23. The material body is meant to experience dualities of blasphemy (*nindana*), praise (*stava*), honor (*satkāra*) and dishonour (*nyakkāra*), which are created due to ignorance, under the influence of external energy.

nindana-stava-satkāra- nyakkārārthaṁ kalevaram
pradhāna-parayo rājann avivekena kalpitam

24. The conditioned soul identifies with the body and its belongings (conception of *mamāham* or 'mine and I'), and thus he is subjected to dualities of praise and chastisement, and considers people to be friends and enemies.

25. But the Supreme Lord has no material body, so He is unaffected by material dualities of praise and blasphemy. His reciprocation with devotees and demons is only for their good.

The Lord's body is nondifferent from Him. As Paramātmā He stays in everyone's body but doesn't identify with the body.

The Lord is unaffected by dualities. He is indifferent to acquisitions. He is not subject to the suffering of being blasphemed and the enjoyment of being praised.

Since the Lord is unaffected by criticism or praise, can one blaspheme Him? – "No! If one criticizes the Lord, he will get bad *karma* (as said in the next verse indirectly)."

26. Somehow, concentrate mind on the Lord	
tasmād vairānubandhena	Therefore, by enmity, or
nirvaireṇa bhayena vā	by devotion or by fear, or
snehāt kāmena vā yuñjyāt	by affection or by lust – one should focus on the Lord
kathañcin nekṣate pṛthak	somehow. He is not affected.

Five types of emotion towards the Lord are mentioned in this verse

- *Vaira* → Continuous enmity that leads to absorption in Kṛṣṇa. *Eg*: Kaṁsa, Śisupāla.
- *Nirvaira* → Without enemity, or with bhakti. *Eg:* Parents of Kṛṣṇa.
- *Bhayena* → Lust with fear. *Eg:* Gopīs who feared rejecting moral codes.
- *Bhayena va* → Lust without fear. *Eg:* Married lover Rukmiṇī.
- *Kāma* → Lust generated by *prema* (*sneha*).

Criticism to absorption: One who criticizes Kṛṣṇa is purified if his critisim leads to continuous remembrance and absorption in the Lord. But if one's criticism doesn't lead to such absorption, it creates bad *karma* and the criticizer goes to hell.

Recommendation: Although the Lord is unaffected by criticism and the criticizer is purified, criticism is not a recommendation. What is recommended is favorable (*anukūla*) devotional service, and not purposeful blasphemy. If uttering the Lord's names with a negative emotion is purifying, then what to speak of favorable chanting?

Two types of criticism of the Lord: (*i*) Favourable and (*ii*) Unfavourable.

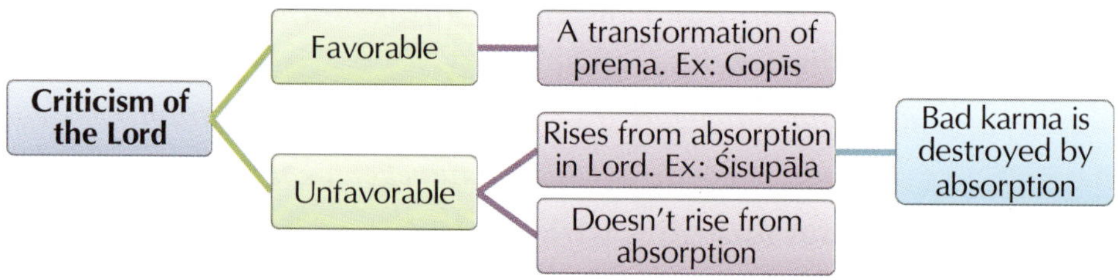

Jaya and Vijaya were ordained to blaspheme Lord for three lives.

27. Enmity leads to more absorption in the Lord than through devotional service.

Nārada's humility: Nārada Muni, being a pure devotee, feels himself deficient in his absorption in Kṛṣṇa, and thus says that the envious demons are more intensely absorbed in the Lord. This, however, shouldn't be taken literally.

Absorption in the thought of Kṛṣṇa is the essential point conveyed in this verse. If an envious mind can be so absorbed in the Lord, what then can be said of a devotee's mind.

28-29. Constant thinking of Kṛṣṇa either with devotion or enmity frees one from all sins and enables one to regain spiritual bodies, just as a grass worm turns into a bee by constant meditation on the bee.

30. Liberation by thinking of Kṛṣṇa in any way	
kāmād dveṣād bhayāt snehād	By lust, hatred, fear and affection
yathā bhaktyeśvare manaḥ	or devotion, thinking of Kṛṣṇa in the mind
āveśya tad-aghaṁ hitvā	with absorption and thus giving up sin or hatred,
bahavas tad-gatiṁ gatāḥ	many attained liberation.

When the mind is somehow or other fully absorbed in Kṛṣṇa, the material part is very soon vanquished and the spiritual part—attraction to Kṛṣṇa—becomes manifest.

The next verse gives examples of personalities who exhibited the emotions towards Kṛṣṇa mentioned in the previous verse.

31. People who attained Kṛṣṇa in various ways	
gopyaḥ kāmād *bhayāt kaṁso*	(*i*) The *gopīs* by conjugal desires for Kṛṣṇa (*ii*) Kaṁsa by fear that Kṛṣṇa will kill him
dveṣāc caidyādayo nṛpāḥ	(*iii*) Śiśupāla and other kings by envy of Kṛṣṇa
sambandhād vṛṣṇayaḥ[2] *snehād yūyaṁ...*	(*iv*) The Yadus and you (the Pāṇḍavas) by affectionate family relation with Kṛṣṇa
...bhaktyā vayaṁ vibho	(*v*) We (general devotees like Nārada) by *bhakti*.

The *kāma* of the *gopīs* is actually *prema* or pure spiritual love for Kṛṣṇa without any material tinges. The *gopīs' kāma* is like gold while Kubja's *kāma* is like iron.

Kaṁsa attained *sāyujya mukti* (merging into the Lord).

Śisupāla, Dantavakra and Paundraka attained *sārūpya mukti* (same form as the Lord).

32. So, somehow concentrate the mind on Kṛṣṇa	
katamo 'pi na venaḥ syāt *pañcānāṁ puruṣaṁ prati*	The atheistic king Vena didn't think of Kṛṣṇa in any of the above five ways, and thus didn't get salvation.
tasmāt kenāpy upāyena	Therefore somehow or the other
manaḥ kṛṣṇe niveśayet	one should focus mind on Lord Kṛṣṇa[3].

Having described the significance of absorption in Kṛṣṇa with love or hatred, Nārada Muni will now address Yudhiṣṭhira Mahārāja's concern in verse 19.

33. Śiśupāla and Dantavakra were formerly associates of Lord Viṣṇu named Jaya and Vijaya. Being cursed by *brāhmaṇas*, they came to this world as demons.

34-48: Nārada Narrates the Curse and Three Births of Jaya and Vijaya

34-35. Mahārāja Yudhiṣṭhira asked, "This is unbelievable. What curse could affect the servants of Lord Viṣṇu (*hari-dāsa*)? They are exclusively dedicated to the Lord and their bodies are purely spiritual. How could they fall to the material world? Please describe the curse that caused this."

---

[2] The word '*vṛṣṇis*' indicates the residents of Vṛndāvana, who had the topmost love for Kṛṣṇa.

[3] Focussing mind on Kṛṣṇa with a favorable mood is the recommendation.

The associates of the Supreme Lord in the spiritual world descend to the material world for the purpose of fulfilling the Lord's desire. Their descent is comparable to Lord's descent and it is an action of spiritual energy. Jaya and Vijaya came to the material world to fulfill the Lord's desire to fight.

36-47: Nārada Muni describes the story of Jaya and Vijaya

36. Once the four Kumāras – Sanaka, Sanandana, Sanātana and Sanat-kumāra – went to Viṣṇu-loka while wandering in the three worlds.

37. They looked like five year old children although they are the eldest sons of Brahmā. Thinking them to be ordinary children, the two gatekeepes of Vaikuṇṭha Jaya and Vijaya forbade them.

38. The Kumāras cursed Jaya and Vijaya, "You are agitated by passion and ignorance, and are unfit to live at the lotus feet of Lord Madhudviṣa. Take birth as demons in the material world."

39. As Jaya and Vijaya were falling, the Kumāras told them kindly, "Your curse will end in three births and you will be able to return to Vaikuṇṭha."

40-43. First birth: Jaya and Vijaya thus descended to the material world as sons of Diti, Hiraṇyakaśipu and Hiraṇyākṣa. They were killed by the Supreme Lord in His incarnations as Nṛsiṁha-deva and Varāha respectively. Hiraṇyakaśipu desired to kill his son Prahlāda and tortured him in many ways. But he couldn't kill Prahlāda, as he was protected by Lord Visṇu, the Supersoul and the equipoised Lord (*sama-darśanam*).

44-45. Second birth: In the next birth, they appeared as Rāvaṇa and Kumbhakarṇa, the sons of Viśravā and Keśinī. The Lord appeared as Rāmacandra and killed them. You may hear narrations about Lord Rāma from Mārkaṇḍeya.

46. Third birth: They appeared as your cousins Śiṣupāla and Dantavakra. Being stuck by the disc of Lord Kṛṣṇa, they are now free from the curse.

47. Salvation by absorption: They maintained a feeling of enmity towards the Lord for a long time. Because of always thinking of Kṛṣṇa in this way they regained the shelter of Lord in Vaikuṇṭha.

vairānubandha-tīvreṇa dhyānenācyuta-sātmatām
nītau punar hareḥ pārśvaṁ jagmatur viṣṇu-pārṣadau

48. Yudhiṣṭhira asked: "Why was there enmity between Hiraṇyakaśipu and his beloved son Prahlāda? How did Prahlāda become such a great devotee of Kṛṣṇa?"

7.2 Hiraṇyakaśipu, King of the Demons

- **1-16:** Hiraṇyakaśipu's reaction after Hiraṇyākṣa's death
  - 1-12: When Hiraṇyākṣa was killed by Varāhadeva, Hiraṇyakaśipu was enraged. He blasphemed Viṣṇu and instructed the demons to persecute brāhmaṇas and destroy Vedic culture. The demons executed his orders.

- **17-61:** Hiraṇyakaśipu consoles his relatives
  - 17-19: After performing the death rites of his brother, Hiraṇyakaśipu spoke to his afflicted relatives.
  - 20-26: Philosophy – "Don't lament, separation is inevitable; Soul is eternal and body is perishable; Bodily identification results in continued material life."
  - 27-36: Story – King Suyajña died in a battle, and his queens didn't allow his deadbody to be burnt.
  - 37-49: Yamarāja comes in the form of a boy and instructs the queens of Suyajña – "The Supreme creator always protects us; The eternal soul is separate form the material body is always invisible; The soul's misidentification leads to bondage and misery; Those who know about the soul do not lament."
  - 50-56: Yamarāja narrates story of Kuliṅga birds – "A hunter captured the female bird and the male bird lamented for her. Meanwhile the hunter killed the male bird too."
  - 57-61: Yamarāja concluded his talk and Suyajña's funeral was performed. Thus, Hiraṇyakaśipu consoled his relatives.

In 7.1.48, Yudhiṣṭhira Mahāraja asked Nārada Muni why Hiraṇyakaśipu was envious of his own son Prahlāda. In this chapter, Nārada Muni narrates the story by explaining how Hiraṇyakaśipu had become a staunch enemy of Lord Viṣṇu.

1-16: Hiraṇyakaśipu's Reaction After Hiraṇyākṣa's Death

1. When Hiraṇyākṣa was killed by Lord Viṣṇu in the form of Varāha, his brother Hiraṇyakaśipu became extremely angry and began to lament.

2-3. Hiraṇyakaśipu was filled with rage. Biting his lips, gazing at the sky with angry eyes, terrible teeth, fierce glances and frowning eyebrows, he spoke to the demons.

4-12: Hiraṇyakaśipu instructs the demons

4-5. "Hear attentively and follow my words without delay, O Śambara, Śatabāhu, Namuci, Vipracitti, Puloman and others!

6. Although Viṣṇu is equal to all (*samena*), He sided the insignificant demigods, being worshiped by them, and killed my obedient and well-wishing brother.

7. Viṣṇu has given up neutrality, being influenced by *māyā*. Just as a restless child takes sides, Viṣṇu, to please His devotees, the demigods, killed my brother in the form of a boar.

8-9. I shall behead that diplomatic Viṣṇu (*kūṭe ahite*) with my trident. With His blood, I shall please my brother who is fond of sucking blood. When He is killed (*naṣṭe*), all the demigods will wither away, just as when a tree's root is cut, the branches and twigs dry up.

Kūṭe ahite indicates that "Viṣṇu has deceptive actions," but it also means "Viṣṇu who fights against cheaters like me."

Naṣṭe can also mean that Viṣṇu becomes invisible, since He cannot be destroyed. The demigods live only for Viṣṇu, who is their life. When He disappears from their sight, they will dry up, out of separation.

Sometimes the demons also appreciate the full dependence of the demigods upon the mercy of the Lord. This is indirect glorification of the demigods by the demons.

10. Meanwhile you destroy all people on the earth engaged in austerity, sacrifice, Vedic study, vows and charity. Earth is flourishing due to *brāhmaṇas*' austerity and *kṣatriya* strength.

11. Lord Viṣṇu has His root in the activities of *dvijas* (*brāhmaṇas* and *kṣatriyas*). He is the personification of sacrifices and religious principles, and the shelter of the demigods, sages, Pitṛs and all beings.

viṣṇur dvija-kriyā-mūlo yajño dharmamayaḥ pumān
devarṣi-pitṛ-bhūtānāṁ dharmasya ca parāyaṇam

Hiraṇyakaśipu's plan: Destruction of *brāhmaṇas* → Destruction of *yajña* and *dharma* → Death of Lord Viṣṇu → Death of demigods.

12. Immediately go destroy places wherever there are cows and *brāhmaṇas*, study of the Vedas, and activities of *varṇāśrama*. Burn the cities and cut down the trees."

13-16: The demons execute Hiraṇyakaśipu's orders

13. The demons started persecuting the citizens, being ordered by their master. They are already fond of such activities (*kadana-priyāḥ*).

14-15. They set fire to cities, villages, gardens, fields, forests, hermitages, cow protectors and even government capitals. They destroyed bridges, city walls and gates, and cut down fruit bearing trees.

16. People were disturbed by them repeatedly and thus gave up Vedic culture. As the sacrifices stopped, the demigods didn't get their oblations and left heaven.

17-61: Hiraṇyakaśipu Consoles His Relatives

17-19. After performing death rites for his brother, Hiraṇyakaśipu tried to pacify his mother Diti, sister-in-law Ruṣābhānu and his nephews Śakuni, Śambara and others. Although angry, being a great politician, he knew how to act according to time and situation. Thus he spoke sweet words as follows.

20-26: Hiraṇyakaśipu speaks philosophy

20. Don't lament for a hero's death, because a great hero's death in front of his enemy is glorious and desirable.

21. Separation is inevitable: The *jīvas* join together in a family by superior arrangement (*daiva*) and get separated by their own *karma*, just as travelers join together at a restaurant and depart to their respective destinations after drinking water.

22a. Qualities of the soul: (*i*) eternal (*nityaḥ*), (*ii*) inexhaustible (*avyayaḥ*), (*iii*) free from material contamination (*śuddhaḥ*), (*iv*) can go anywhere in the material or spiritual worlds (*sarva-gaḥ*), (*v*) full of knowledge (*sarva-vit*) and (*vi*) different from the body (*paraḥ*).

22b. Cause of entanglement: But because of ignorance and misuse of his slight independence, the soul accepts subtle and gross bodies created by the material energy and thus subjected to so-called material happiness and distress.

23. Examples

- **A tree seems to move** when reflected in moving water.
- **The land apears to move** when the eyes move due to some mental derangement.

24. Bodily identification (liṅga-bhāvanā): Similarly, when the mind is agitated by the movement of modes, the soul, although pure and freed from subtle and gross bodies (*aliṅgaḥ*), thinks that he is identical with those bodies (*liṅga-vān*).

25-26. Result of misidentification: In such a bewildered state, the *jīva* discriminates between people as friends and enemies and thus enjoys or suffers in various material bodies. This continued material life is called *saṁsāra*. Birth, death, lamentation, foolishness and anxiety are due to such material considerations.

27-36: Hiraṇyakaśipu narrates the story of Suyajña

27-28. Old story: In this regard, there is an old historical example of a discourse by Yamarāja to the relatives of a dead person. Please hear attentively. Suyajña was the king of Uśīnara. When he was killed in a battle, his kinsmen began to lament.

29-30. The slain King Suyajña fell with his bejewelled armor smashed, ornaments fallen, hair scattered, eyes lustreless, body smeared with blood, heart pierced by arrows, teeth still biting his lips, face covered with dust and arms broken.

31-32. His queens cried seeing him thus killed by fate (*vidhinā*): "O lord, now that you are killed, we are also killed." They fell at his feet with tears, pounding their breasts. Their hair disarrayed and ornaments fell. All this evoked sympathy of others.

33-34. The queens lamented saying –

- **"You were the maintainer** of Uśīnara, and now you increase the lamentation of its population. O lord, the cruel providence has taken you away from our sight.
- **You were a grateful husband** and our most sincere friend. We cannot exist without you. We will follow you (we will die – *saha-maraṇa*) and serve you."

35-36. They didn't allow the dead body to be burnt even though the sun was about to set. Their cries reached the abode of Yamarāja, who then personally came in the form of boy to advice them.

Verses 37-57 describe the instructions of Yamarājā to the queens of Sujajña.

37-49: Yamarāja instructs the queens of Suyajña about the eternal soul

37. Alas, it is amazing that these people, older than me, who have seen thousands of births and deaths are still bewildered. After death, one goes to an unknown place from where he has come. There is no exception to this. Why to lament uselessly?

38. We are fortunate because, though we are children, very weak and unprotected by parents, we have not been eaten by ferocious animals. The Supreme Lord who protected us in the womb of mother will protect us everywhere.

Yamarāja thus expresses his wonder in the above two verses by comparing himself (a young boy) with the queens who are much older than himself.

39. By the Supreme Lord's will only is the world created, maintained and destroyed. This world of moving and non-moving beings, is simply a plaything for Him, who is fully competent to destroy and protect (*nigraha-saṅgrahe prabhuḥ*).

40. By the Supreme Lord's protection, even lost money could be recovered and an unsheltered person could survive in the forest. But without His mercy, money that is securely maintained could also be lost and a well-protected person at home could die.

But is that the inequality in the Lord, because He favors one and ignores another?

41. The soul is different from the material bodies in different species that appear and disappear by the *karmas* of the *jīva*.

42. But the soul identifies with the body due to ignorance, just as a householder thinks himself to be identical to the house although he is different.

43. The soul is separate from the body just as –

- Fire is separate from wood although situated within it
- Air is separate although situated within the mouth and nostrils
- Sky never mixes with anything, although all-pervading

Still the relatives of a dead person cannot understand this.

44. The actual person is invisible: Your lamentation is contradictory, O fools! The person named Suyajña, for whom you lament, is still lying before you. You have never seen the person within the body who heard you and replied.

45. Soul and Supersoul: The life air in the body is most important, yet it is also not the listener or the speaker. Beyond the life air is the soul who is the possessor of the senses. The soul is directed by the Supersoul, the ultimate proprietor of all senses.

46. By his own power (*svena tejasā*) or knowledge, the *jīva* accepts and gives up higher and lower material bodies made of the five elements, ten senses and the mind.

The *jīva* has the freewill to either follow higher spiritual instructions and go to the spiritual world or choose to remain in the material world.

47. Bondage and misery: As long as the soul is covered by subtle body (*liṅgānvito*), he is bound to the results of his fruitive acts (*karma-nibandhanam*). That bondage leads to miseries and a strong relationship with *māyā*.

48. It is a fruitless misconception (*vitathābhiniveśo*) to see and talk of the effects of modes as if they are permanent. Just as mental concoctions (*manorathā*) and dreams (*svapna*) are insubstantial, the happiness and distress produced by material senses (*aindriyakam*) are meaningless (*mṛṣā*).

49. Those who are in knowledge of the eternal soul (*nityam*) and perishable body (*anityam*) do not lament. Others are prone to lamentation. It is difficult to educate them.

Despite being enlightened by Yamarāja (in the form of a boy), the wives of King Suyajña didn't stop their lamentation. So Yamarāja then narrated the following story.

50-56: Yamarāja narrates story of Kuliṅga birds

50-52. A hunter captured the female bird: Once there lived a hunter as if appointed by death personified as the killer of the birds in the forest. Once he saw a pair of *kuliṅga* birds and captured the female bird by his lure. Seeing his wife in danger and beig unable to release her, the male bird lamented.

53-55. The male kuliṅga bird lamented:

- **Providence is merciless.** What will Providence gain by putting my wife in this awkward position.
- **Let Him take me also.** My wife is half of my body, what is the use of my living with only half body?
- **The baby birds are helpless.** How shall I maintain them who haven't developed wings?

56. The hunter killed the male bird with an arrow as he was lamenting.

57. Yamaraj concludes: O foolish women, even if you lament for hundreds of years, your husband will not be alive, and in the meantime your lives will be finished.

58-59. Everyone was struck with wonder at the instructions of Yamarāja, in the form of a boy. Yamarāja disappeared and Suyajña's relatives did his funeral ceremony.

60. Hiraṇyakaśipu concludes: Therefore do not be aggrieved for loss of body.

61. Nārada Muni concludes: After hearing the instructions, Diti and others forgot their grief.

7.3 Hiraṇyakaśipu's Plan to Become Immortal

- **1-5:** Hiraṇyakaśipu's desires, austerities and their effects
  - 1: Desires: to be – unconquerable, free from old age, deathless, without rival etc.
  - 2: Austerities: at Mt. Mandara, standing on toes, keeping arms upward and looking toward the sky.
  - 3-5: Effects of austerities: Fire emanated from his head, spread everywhere, and heated up all planets; the globe trembled.
- **6-13:** The demigods' appeal to Lord Brahmā
  - 6-8: Please stop these disturbances
  - 9-11: Hiraṇyakaśipu's plans – to occupy the post of Brahmā and reverse the established dharma in the world
  - 12-13: Please take suitable action
- **14-38:** Lord Brahmā gives benedictions to Hiraṇyakaśipu
  - 14-21: Brahmā goes to Hiraṇyakaśipu, appreciates his determination and promises to offer boons
  - 22-25: Brahmā enlivens the emaciated body of Hiraṇyakaśipu
  - 26-34: Hiraṇyakaśipu offers obeisances and glorifies Brahmā
  - 35-38: Hiraṇyakaśipu asks benedctions from Lord Brahmā

Having consoled his relatives, Hiraṇyakaśipu goes to do austerities to become immortal.

1-5: Hiraṇyakaśipu's Desires, Austerities and Their Effects

1. Hiraṇyakaśipu's desired to be – (*i*) unconquerable (*ajeyam*), (*ii*) free from old age (*ajara*), (*iii*) deathless (*amaram*), (*iv*) without rival (*apratidvandvam*) and (*v*) the sole king of the entire universe (*eka-rājam*).

With these desires Hiraṇyakaśipu goes to perform austerities.

2. Hiraṇyakaśipu did severe austerities in the valley of Mandara mountain by – (*i*) standing on his toes, (*ii*) keeping his arms upward and (*iii*) looking toward the sky.

3-5. Effect of Hiraṇyakaśipu's austerities

i. Light emanated from his locks of hair as the sunrays during dissolution
ii. Wandering demigods returned to their homes
iii. Fire emanated from his head and spread everywhere and heated up all planets
iv. All the rivers and oceans were agitated
v. The surface of the globe, with its mountains and islands, began trembling
vi. The stars and planets fell
vii. All directions were ablaze

Disturbed by Hiraṇyakaśipu's severe austerities, all the demigods left their planets and went to the planet of Lord Brahmā, the creator, and informed him as follows.

6-13: The Demigods' Appeal to Lord Brahmā

6-8. Please stop these disturbances: O lord of the demigods! O master of the universe! We are scorched and unable to stay in our planets. If you think it proper, kindly stop these disturbances, before your obedient citizens are annihilated. Although you might know, please hear of Hiraṇyakaśipu's intentions behind his austerities.

9-11. Please hear Hiraṇyakaśipu's plans:

- "I will occupy Brahmā's post. Brahmā got his exalted post by austerities (*tapa*), mystic power (*yoga*) and trance (*samādhi*) and became most worshipable demigod in the universe. I shall endeavor in a similar way and occupy his post, since I (the soul) am eternal and time is eternal. I prefer this to even Dhruvaloka.
- I shall reverse the results of pious and impious activities.
- I shall over turn all the established practices within this world."

12-13. Please take suitable action: Your post is most auspicious for everyone in the universe, especially for the cows and *brāhmaṇas*, for material happiness and opulence. But if that demon takes your position, everything will be lost.

14-38: Lord Brahmā Gives Benedictions to Hiraṇyakaśipu

14-16. Brahmā went to see Hiraṇyakaśipu, along with Bhṛgu, Dakṣa and other sages. Brahmā initially couldn't see Hiraṇyakaśipu, whose body was covered by an anthill, grass and bamboo. The ants had devoured his skin, fat, flesh and blood. Spotting him, struck with wonder, Brahmā smiled and spoke to him.

17-21: Lord Brahmā addresses Hiraṇyakaśipu

17. Perfect: Now you are perfect in austerities. Ask from me whatever you desire.

18. Astonishing: Its astonishing to see your endurance. In spite of being eaten by all kinds of insects, your life air is circulating within your bones.

19. Unparallelled: Previous great sages like Bhṛgu also could not do such austerities, nor will anyone in the future will. Who can sustain his life without even water for 100 celestial years?

20. Conquered: Your determination and unprecedented austerity have conquered me.

21. Boons: I will give you all benedictions. Your audience with me will not go in vain.

22-25: Hiraṇyakaśipu gets revived

22-23. Brahmā enlivened Hiraṇyakaśipu by sprinkling upon him divine water from his *kamaṇḍalu*. Hiraṇyakaśipu arose as a young man with body as strong as thunderbolt, and lustre resembling molten gold.

24-25. Hiraṇyakaśipu was pleased seeing Lord Brahmā and fell flat on the ground. Rising up, he was overwhelmed by jubilation. With tears in his eyes and hairs standing on end, he prayed in a faltering voice.

26-34: Hiraṇyakaśipu glorifies Lord Brahmā

Although Hiraṇyakaśipu praises Brahmā in this section as if he were the Supreme Lord, it is Lord Kṛṣṇa who is the original creator and master of this cosmic manifestation. Brahmā is only the secondary creator. Lord Kṛṣṇa empowers Brahmā as the engineer to create this phenomenal world. Thus the following glories should actually be attributed to Lord Kṛṣṇa.

26-27. Obeisances unto the great, supreme and self-effulgent lord Brahmā who is the shelter of the three modes. When the universe is covered by darkness by the influence of time at the end of his day, he manifests it again by his own effulgence, maintains it and destroys it, by the modes.

28-33: Hiraṇyakaśipu praises Lord Brahmā as –	
28	• Original personality within this universe (*ādya*) • The seed of cosmos (*bīja*) • The form of knowledge and realization (*jñāna-vijñāna-mūrtaye*) • One who applies mind and realized intelligence in creating this cosmos
29	• Controller of all moving and non-moving living entities by the chief prāṇa • Master of all living entities (*patiḥ prajānām*) • Maintainer of the mind and senses • Lord of all the material elements and their qualities, and all desires
30	• Propagator of seven kinds of sacrifices, headed by agniṣṭoma by the three Vedas and four kinds of priests (*hotā, udghātā, adhvaryū* and *brahma*) • Supreme Soul of all beings, beginningless, endless and omniscient
31	• Eternally awake, seeing everything that happens • Eternal time that reduces the life span of all living entities • Changeless, witness, unborn, great, all-pervading, cause of life for all
32	• Not separate from anything, be it better or lower, stationary or moving • Has body formed by knowledge of scriptures • Hiraṇyagarbha, containing the universe in belly • Greatest and transcendental to the world of three modes
33	• Universal form in this world, although situted in his own abode • Brahman, the Supersoul, the oldest Lord
34	• Pervades the universe with an unlimited and unmanifested form • Endowed with material and spiritual energies

Anticipating Brahmā's inability to bestow immortality, as Brahmā himself is not immortal, Hiraṇyakaśipu cleverly asks a benediction to avoid death.

35-38: Hiraṇyakaśipu asks benedctions from Lord Brahmā	
35-37a	**Let me not meet death –** • from any of the living entities created by you • within or outside of any residence • during the daytime or at night, on the ground or in the sky • by any others beyond you, by any weapon, human being or animal • from any living or nonliving entity • by any demigod or demon or snakes from the lower planets
37b	• Let me not have any rival.
38a	• Give me sole lordship over all the living entities and presiding deities
38b	• Give me all the mystic powers attained by long austerities and *yoga* practice

7.4 Hiraṇyakaśipu Terrorizes The Universe

- **1-20:** Hiraṇyakaśipu's nefarious activities after receiving boons
  - 1-3: Brahmā grants the benedictions asked by Hiraṇyakaśipu and departs
  - 4-14: Hiraṇyakaśipu's envy, influence, oppression of the demigods, intoxication and receiving everyone's worship
  - 15-18: Hiraṇyakaśipu usurps sacrificial shares and controls nature
  - 19-20: Hiraṇyakaśipu's uncontrolled senses, dissatisfaction and pride
- **21-29:** The demigods approach Lord Viṣṇu for protection
  - 21-23: In distress and fear of Hiraṇyakaśipu, the demigods worship Lord Hriṣīkeśa
  - 24-29: The demigods hear the Lord's reassuring voice – "Do not fear. I am there. I shall stop Hiraṇyakaśipu's evil acts when he teases his noble son Prahlāda"
- **30-43:** Transcendental qualities of Prahlāda Mahārāja
  - 30-37: Prahlāda was self-controlled, determined, respectful to elders, affectionate to the equals, kind to the poor, surrendered to the wise, prideless, unagitated, naturally attached to the Lord, and uninterested in externals
  - 38-43: Being always embraced by Lord Govinda, Prahlāda exhibits symptoms of ecstasy but Hiraṇyakaśipu torments him
- **44-46:** Yudhiṣṭira Mahārāja inquires from Nārada Muni
  - "How did Hiraṇyakaśipu give so much trouble to his saintly son Prahlāda? Parents are affectionate and chastise children only to instruct them, but not out of enmity!"

This chapter describes – (*i*) how Hiraṇyakaśipu misuses his power gained by austerities and defeats the demigods due to hatred for Lord Viṣṇu, and (*ii*) Prahlāda's qualities that arose from his *prema-bhaki*.

1-20: Hiraṇyakaśipu's Nefarious Activities After Receiving Boons

1-2. Lord Brahmā granted benedictions asked by the demon Hiraṇyakaśipu, being satisfied with difficult austerities. He said, "Although these benedictions are difficult to obtain (*durlabhān*), I shall grant you those rare boons."

Durlabhān: Material benedictions are exactly not worthy of being called benedictions, for they could become curses. Just as it takes great endeavor to acquire those boons, it is difficult to maintain them as well. Thus, although Hiraṇyakaśipu attained great boons from Brahmā, they are still not attained (*durlabhān*).

3. Brahmā then departed being worshiped by Hiraṇyakaśipu and praised by sages.

4. Hiraṇyakaśipu's envy: He acquired a lustrous golden body by Brahmā's boons. He remembered the death of his brother and continued to be envious of Lord Viṣṇu.

5-7. Hiraṇyakaśipu's influence: He conquered all directions and planets in the three worlds including that of the human beings, the demigods, the serpents, the Garuḍas and so on. Conquering the abodes of all, he seized their power and influence.

8-11. Hiraṇyakaśipu resided in Indra's heavenly palace (*mahendra-bhavana*), built by Viśvakarmā and endowed with all opulences and beautiful celestial gardens. That palace has – (*i*) steps made of coral (*ii*) floor bedecked with emeralds (*iii*) walls made of crystal (*iv*) columns with *vaidūrya* (*v*) colorful canopies (*vi*) seats bedecked with rubies (*vii*) silk bedding as white as foam decorated with pearls and (*vii*) ladies with beautiful faces, teeth and ankle bells tinkling melodiously, who saw their own beautiful reflections in the gems.

12. He oppressed the demigods, who had to bow at his feet. As a powerful conqueror, dictator (*eka-rāṭ*) and severe ruler (*caṇḍa-śāsana*), he chastised them for no reason.

Even in the higher planetary systems, to which people are promoted by pious activities, disturbances are created by demons like Hiraṇyakaśipu. No one in the three worlds can live in peace and prosperity without disturbance. In the material world, sometimes even great personalities can be controled by demons (as will be seen in *Verse* 14).

13a. He was always intoxicated with his eyes rolling.

13b. Everyone worshipped him because of his austerity (*tapa*), *yoga*, physical and sensual strength (*bala* and *ojas*). Except Brahmā, Viṣṇu and Śiva, the principal men of all planets offered him presentations with their own hands.

14. Everyone offered him prayers, including the two Gandharvas Viśvāvasu and Tumburu, I myself (Nārada) and the Vidyādharas, Apsarās and sages.

15. He usurped sacrificial shares (*havir-bhāgān*) for himself, offered by the strict followers of *varṇāśrama*.

16-18. Hiraṇyakaśipu controls nature

- **Earth** delivered abundant food grains without being plowed, like a *surabhī* cow
- **Cows** supplied abundant milk
- **The outer space** was decorated with wonderful phenomena
- **The seven oceans** (of salt water, wine, ghee, sugarcane juice, yoghurt, milk and sweet water) of the universe along with rivers (their wives) supplied various kinds of gems and jewels.
- **Mountains and valleys** became fields of pleasure for Hiraṇyakaśipu.
- **Trees** and plants produced fruits and flowers profusely in all seasons.
- He alone performed the functions of all the demigods.

19. Yet dissatisfied: In spite of controlling all directions and enjoying all kinds of sense gratification, he was dissatisfied due to uncontrolled senses (*ajitendriyaḥ*).

sa itthaṁ nirjita-kakub eka-rāḍ viṣayān priyān
yathopajoṣaṁ bhuñjāno nātṛpyad ajitendriyaḥ

20. He thus passed a long time being proud of his opulence (*aiśvarya-matta*), and transgressing the scriptural rules (*ut-śāstra-vartina*), being subjected to the curse of the Kumāras (*brahma-śāpam*).

The word *śāstra* refers to that which controls our activities. We cannot violate or transgress the principles mentioned in the *śāstras*. The material energy is so powerful that as soon as one becomes materially opulent, he begins to transgress the *śāstric* laws and thus enters upon the path of destruction.

21-29: The Demigods Approach Lord Viṣṇu for Protection

21. Everyone was distressed by the severe punishments of Hiraṇyakaśipu. The demigods in fear and distress at last took shelter (*śaraṇam*) of Lord Viṣṇu (Acyuta).

Supreme shelter: In distress, one wants to seek shelter of a well-wishing friend. The well-wishing friend of the perfect order is Lord Śrī Kṛṣṇa. If from the very beginning we seek His shelter, there will be no cause of danger. Seeking shelter of demigods and others is like trying to cross the ocean by catching a dog's tail.

22-23. The demigods worshiped Lord Hṛṣīkeśa with controlled minds, without sleep and living only on their breath. They prayed, "Obeisances to the direction where the

Supersoul and the Supreme controller, Lord Hari is situated, where the purified peaceful *sannyāsīs* go, and from where one does not return."

Lord Hari is there in every direction, in every heart and in every atom. Yet the demigods offer respects to the direction where Lord Hari stays. At that time, Hiraṇyakaśipu's influence was everywhere except the specific places (*dhāmas*) where the Supreme Lord had His pastimes.

24. Then they heard a voice from a personality invisible to material eyes. It was –

i. As grave as the rumbling of a cloud (*megha-niḥsvanā*)
ii. Resounding in all directions (*sannādayantī kakubhaḥ*)
iii. Encouraging, driving away the fear of saintly persons (*sādhūnām abhayaṅkarī*)

25-28: Message of the Supreme Lord to the demigods

25. Do not fear, I am there	
mā bhaiṣṭa vibudha-śreṣṭhāḥ	Do not fear, O best of learned persons!
sarveṣāṁ bhadram astu vaḥ	I wish all good fortune to you.
mad-darśanaṁ hi bhūtānāṁ sarva-śreyopapattaye	Seeing Me[4] (by hearing and chanting about Me and offering prayers) gives highest benefit to all beings.

By "*mad-darśanam*" the Lord indicates that the demigods will suffer only till they see Him coming out of the pillar as Nṛsimhadeva.

26. I shall stop Hiraṇyakaśipu's evil acts which are known to Me. Please patiently wait for the time when I will appear.

27. Envious person is vanquished	
yadā deveṣu vedeṣu	When – towards (*i*) the demigods (*ii*) the Vedas
goṣu vipreṣu sādhuṣu	(*iii*) the cows (*iv*) *brāhmaṇas* (*v*) Vaiṣṇavas and
dharme mayi ca vidveṣaḥ	(*vi*) religious principles – one shows envy,
sa vā āśu vinaśyati	he and his civilization will be vanquished.

The above things represent the Supreme Lord and when one is envious of them, he is ultimately envying the Lord.

---

[4] **Mad-darśanam:** The ability to understand the Lord or to see Him or talk with Him depends on one's advancement in *bhakti* or devotional service (*bhaktyā mām abhijānāti*).

28. When Hiraṇyakaśipu teases his son Prahlāda, who is (*i*) without enemy (*nrivaira*), (*ii*) peaceful (*praśānta*) and (*iii*) a great devotee (*mahātma*), – I shall kill him, despite the benedictions of Brahmā.

Vaiṣṇava-aparādha: The Supreme Lord can tolerate anything, but not violence towards His devotees. Of all sinful activities, an offense to a Vaiṣṇava is the most severe. All the benedictions received by an offender would be null and void as soon as he commits an offense at the lotus feet of a deovtee.

A Vaiṣṇava is *nirvaira*, he has no enemies (See 3.25.21 also)

29. Thus being reassured by the Lord, the supreme spiritual master (*loka-guru*), the demigods offered respects and returned, considering that the demon is already dead.

Even the demigods also approach the Supreme Lord Viṣṇu when harassed by demons. So, it is better to approach the Supreme Lord for whatever benefits one desires, instead of approaching the demigods (See 2.3.10).

30-43: Transcendental Qualities of Prahlāda Mahārāja

30. Hiraṇyakaśipu had four wonderful sons. The best of them was Prahlāda, the reservoir of transcendental qualities, because he was an unalloyed devotee of Viṣṇu.

A devotee of the Supreme Lord Viṣṇu or Kṛṣṇa is endowed with all good qualities, both material and spiritual. (See 5.18.12).

31-32. Qualities of Prahlāda		
i	*brahmaṇyaḥ*	Qualified as a *brāhmaṇa* and Devoted to spiritual knowledge
ii	*śīla-sampannaḥ*	Endowed with good character
iii	*satya-sandho*	Determined to understand the Absolute Truth and true to his promise
iv	*jitendriyaḥ*	Has full control of mind and senses
v	*ātmavat sarva-bhūtānām eka-priya-suhṛttamaḥ*	Like the Paramātmā, he is kind to all beings and their one dear best friend and well-wisher
vi	*dāsavat sannatāryāṅghriḥ*	Surrendered to feet of the wise like a menial servant
vii	*pitṛvad dīna-vatsalaḥ*	Kind to the poor like a father
viii	*bhrātṛvat sadṛśe snigdho*	Affectionate to equals like a brother
ix	*guruṣv īśvara-bhāvanaḥ*	Respectful to *gurus* seeing them as good as the Lord
x	*vidyārtha-rūpa-janmāḍhyo*	Endowed with education, wealth, beauty, good birth
xi	*māna-stambha-vivarjitaḥ*	Free of pride and unsubmissiveness

33. Further qualities of Prahlāda		
i	*nodvigna-citto vyasaneṣu*	Unagitated when put into dangers
ii	*niḥspṛhaḥ śruteṣu dṛṣṭeṣu guṇeṣv*	Not desirous of hearing or seeing sense objects or Vedic fruitive acts
iii	*avastu-dṛk*	Saw the world as insubstantial
iv	*dāntendriya-prāṇa-śarīra-dhīḥ sadā*	Always controlled his senses, life air, body and intelligence
v	*praśānta-kāmo*	He subdued all lusty desires
vi	*rahitāsuro 'suraḥ*	Although born in family of demons, he was devoid of demoniac qualities such as envy

Birth Vs. qualities: A man is not qualified or disqualified by birth. Prahlāda was born in a family of demons, but he has all the qualities of a perfect *brāhmaṇa*. He provided a vivid example of how to think of the spiritual master and accept his directions.

34. God's qualities in a devotee: The wise glorify Prahlāda's divine qualities (*mahad-guṇā*): "All good qualities of the Supreme Lord exist forever in His devotee Prahlāda."

The Lord exists simultaneously in different places – in His Planet Goloka Vṛndāvana and in the core of everyone's heart. Similarly Prahlāda still lives in Vaikuṇṭhaloka as well as within this material world on the planet Sutala. A devotee can be qualified like the Supreme Personality of Godhead, not in full but partially. The similarity in qualities of the Lord and His devotees can be perceived only by wise men.

35. In saintly assemblies (*sadhu-gāthā-sadasi*), even the demigods cite Prahlāda as an example of a great devotee (*praimānam*), what to speak of you?

36a. Prahlāda's innumerable qualities cannot be listed. He is a great soul (*mahātma*).

36b. Prahlāda had natural attachment towards Lord Vāsudeva (*vāsudeve bhagavati yasya naisargikī ratiḥ*), i.e., his attraction did not develop by *sādhana* over many births as is the case with others.

Here the word '*vāsudeva*' could refer to Narasiṁha or Kṛṣṇa (See 7.4.37) or Govinda (See 7.4.38)

37. Absorption in Kṛṣṇa; Disinterest in externals		
i	*nyasta-krīḍanako bālo*	He was uninterested in childish playthings
ii	*jaḍavat tan-manastayā*	He seemed to be dull, being fully absorbed in Kṛṣṇa
iii	*kṛṣṇa-graha-gṛhītātmā*	His mind was completely overcome by Kṛṣṇa
iv	*na veda jagad īdṛśam*	He could not understand how this world goes on, being fully absorbed in the activities of sense enjoyment

A *mahā-bhāgavata* devotee sees Kṛṣṇa everywhere because of his attitude of pure love for Kṛṣṇa. Everything appears yellow to the jaundiced eye, similarly, to a *mahā-bhāgavata*, everyone but himself appears to be engaged in Kṛṣṇa's service.

38. Being always embraced by Govinda (*govinda-parirambhitaḥ*), Prahlāda was not aware of his actions of sitting, walking, eating, lying down, drinking and talking.

Just as a one year old baby is constantly embraced on the lap of its mother, Prahlāda was embraced by the Lord while doing all his activities. No one else saw the Lord.

39-41. Prahlāda's symptoms of ecstasy: Sometimes Prahlāda would –

- **Cry** (*rudati*) when his mind was troubled (*śabala-cetanaḥ*) due to Lord's absence
- **Laugh** (*hasati*) upon seeing the Lord again
- **Be joyful** on thinking of the Lord (*tat-cintā-hlādaḥ*) and **sing** loudly (*udgāyati*)
- **Loudly call** out (*nadati*) the Lord in full **anxiety** (*utkaṇṭha*)
- **Dance** in jubilation without shyness
- **Imitate** (*anucakāra*) the Lord's pastimes, being absorbed in His thoughts (*tad-bhāvanā-yukta*) and feeling oneness with Him (*tanmaya*)
- **Be silent** (*tūṣṇīm*) with hairs standing on end (*utpulakas*)
- **Feel the touch** of the Lord's hands and become **blissful** (*saṁsparśa-nirvṛtaḥ*)
- **Not move** and shed tears from his half-closed eyes due to his love for the Lord

42. Power of good association	
sa uttama-śloka-padāravindayor niṣevayākiñcana-saṅga-labdhayā	By his association with pure devotees who had nothing to do with anything material, Prahlāda constantly engaged in service of Lord's lotus feet
tanvan parāṁ nirvṛtim ātmano muhur	Prahlāda constantly inspired highest transcendental bliss
duḥsaṅga-dīnasya manaḥ śamaṁ vyadhāt	By seeing his ecstatic bodily features, persons very poor in spiritual understanding became purified

Bhakti is unconditional: Although Prahlāda was born in the family of demons and tortured by his own father, he had no danger from such bad association. He had an undisturbed mind and steady *bhakti*, and even influenced others to absorb their minds in the Supreme Lord. This proves that *bhakti* is never interrupted (*ahaituky apratihatā*) by material conditions.

43. Hiraṇyakaśipu tormented Prahlāda, the broad-minded (*mahātma*), fortunate (*mahā-bhāga*) and exalted devotee (*mahā-bhāgavata*), although he was his own son.

One who oppresses a pure devotee loses all the results of his austerities, penances and pious activities.

44-46: Yudhiṣṭhira Mahārāja Inquires From Nārada Muni

44. How did Hiraṇyakaśipu give so much trouble to his pure (*śuddha*) and saintly (*sādhu*) son Prahlāda? O best of spiritual leaders, I wish to know about this.

45. Parents are affectionate to their children. They chastise if children are disobedient or naughty, but it is for their instruction and not out of enmity.

46. How was it possible for a father to be so violent to his obedient, respectful and well-behaved son? Kindly dissipate our doubts in this regard.

7.5 Prahlāda Mahārāja the Saintly Son of Hiraṇyakaśipu

- **1-32:** Prahlāda's devotion to Viṣṇu and Hiraṇyakaśipu's response
  - 1-3: Prahlāda's education under Śukrācārya's sons
  - 4-10: Prahlāda instructs Hiraṇyakaśipu in bhakti
  - 11-18: Śaṇḍa and Amarka chastise Prahlāda and forcefully teach him
  - 19-24: Prahlāda describes the nine processes of bhakti to Hiraṇyakaśipu
  - 25-29: Hiraṇyakaśipu becomes angry and asks Prahlāda who taught him this knowledge
  - 30-32: Prahlāda describes the nature and destination of householders, and the power of serving a Vaiṣṇava
- **33-44:** Hiraṇyakaśipu's attempts to kill Prahlāda
  - 33-38: Hiraṇyakaśipu orders his servants to kill Prahlāda
  - 39-44: Hiraṇyakaśipu fails to kill Prahlāda through elephants, snakes, poison and so on. Prahlāda's meditation on Viṣṇu was undisturbed.
- **45-57:** Prahlāda sent to school again
  - 45-47: Hiraṇyakaśipu suspects his own death because of his enmity towards Prahlāda
  - 48-52: Śaṇḍa and Amarka told Hiraṇyakaśipu that Prahlāda might change later, and Prahlāda was again sent to school
  - 53-57: Prahlāda begins to enlighten his schoolmates

In respose to Yudhiṣṭhira Mahārāja's questions in 7.4.44-46, Nārada Muni explains how Hiraṇyakaśipu became so violent towards Prahlāda.

1-32: Prahlāda's Devotion to Viṣṇu and Hiraṇyakaśipu's Response

1-3: Prahlāda's education under Śukrācārya's sons

1. The demons accepted Śukrācārya as their priest for rituals (*paurohitya*). His two sons, Śaṇḍa and Amarka, lived near Hiraṇyakaśipu's palace.

Śukrācārya accepted the priesthood of demons for material benefits. A real *brāhmaṇa* should become priest of a person interested in spiritual advancement, not atheistic men.

2. Prahlāda was sent for education to Śaṇḍa and Amarka, along with other boys born of demons, although Prahlāda was already knowledgeable in politics, morals and devotion (*naya-kovidān*).

3. Prahlāda didn't like political philosophy taught by his teachers, since it involved thinking in terms of duality of oneself and others (*sva-para*) or enemy and friend.

A devotee sees everyone as part and parcel of the Supreme Lord Kṛṣṇa. He never creates a situation of material friendship and enmity with others.

4-10: Prahlāda instructs Hiraṇyakaśipu in bhakti

4. Once Hiraṇyakaśipu asked Prahlāda affectionately, taking him on his lap: "Please tell me what you consider to be the best of all subjects (*manyate sādhu yad bhavān*)."

A devotee sees everyone as part and parcel of the Supreme Lord Kṛṣṇa. He never creates a situation of material friendship and enmity with others.

5. Prahlāda's reply: "Give up family life and take shelter of Hari"	
tat sādhu manye 'sura-varya dehināṁ	O best of the demons, I think the best thing for all the embodied beings
sadā samudvigna-dhiyām asad-grahāt	who are always full of anxieties, with minds absorbed in "I and mine" conception is –
hitvātma-pātaṁ gṛham andha-kūpaṁ	to give up the soul degrading, blind-well like materialistic household life, and
vanaṁ gato yad dharim āśrayeta	go to forest (Vṛndāvana) and take shelter of the Supreme Lord Hari.

Hiraṇyakaśipu expected something pleasing to hear from Prahlāda, but nothing practical. He was surprised to hear such profound words from his young son.

6-7. Hiraṇyakaśipu laughed and said, "The intelligence of children is being spoiled by the words of the enemy (*para-pakṣa*). Protect this boy at *guru-kula* from the Vaiṣṇavas who may go there in disguise as *brāhmaṇas*."

Prahlāda's teachers were astonished to see that a small boy could speak such exalted Vaiṣṇava philosophy. So they inquired from him about the Vaiṣṇavas who stealthily taught him, so that they could be arrested and killed by Hiraṇyakaśipu.

8-10. Śaṇḍa and Amarka asked Prahlāda mildly after coming back to *guru-kula:* "All good fortune unto you. Please speak the truth. Other boys do not speak like you. How have you learned these instructions? Who polluted your intelligence?"

Prahlāda will now respond that his intelligence has not been polluted. By the grace of his *guru* (Nārada Muni), he learnt that no one is his friend or enemy. Everyone is an eternal servant of Lord Kṛṣṇa.

11-14: Prahlāda answers the question of Śaṇḍa and Amarka

11. Māyā's effect: The Lord's *māyā* has created the material conception of life (*asad-grāhaḥ*) that distinguishes people as 'friends' and 'enemies' (*sva-para*), by deluding the intelligence (*vimohita-dhiyāṁ*) of men. My respects to that Supreme Lord.

12. Lord's grace: When God is pleased with someone, – (*i*) one's animal intelligence (*paśu-buddhi*) is destroyed and (*ii*) one doesn't make distinctions of friends and enemies.

Duality: As long as one adheres to the philosophy of duality, thinking one person a friend and another an enemy, he is in the clutches of *māyā*.

Oneness: Every living entity is a part and parcel of Lord Kṛṣṇa. Kṛṣṇa is the well-wisher of all *jīvas* and all *jīvas* are His eternal servants. Thus they are all one.

Vaiṣṇava thinking or Vaikuṇṭha thinking is to be friendly with other servants of the Lord and appreciate their service, and not be proud of one's own service. There may be apparent competition amongst the servants, but there is no envy. Everyone is allowed to serve the Lord to the best of one's ability.

Distinction: The *jīvas* and the Lord are one in spiritual indentity, but the *jīvas* are not equal to God as the Māyāvādīs think. No one is equal to God. The servant cannot be equal to the master. Their distinction must continue even in the liberated stage.

13. My intelligence is different from yours due to the Lord, your so-called enemy. People with faulty intelligence (*abuddhibhiḥ*) see in terms of oneself and others, and cannot ascertain the Supersoul. Even the knowers of the Vedas like Brahmā are sometimes bewildered (what to speak of you?).

14. My consciousness is naturally attracted to Lord Viṣṇu (Cakrapāṇi, who holds the disc) just as iron is naturally attracted to a magnet. Thus I have no independence.

Kṛṣṇa means one who attracts everyone. To be attracted to Kṛṣṇa is the natural position of every living entity. There is no cause or goal in such attraction and it is not induced by anything external. The highest examples of such attraction are the Vrajavāsis.

Due to material contamination one may not be attracted to Kṛṣṇa, but once one is purified of that contamination by the practice of *bhakti,* one is again attracted to Kṛṣṇa.

15-18: Śaṇḍa and Amarka chastise and teach Prahlāda

15. Śaṇḍa and Amarka became angry and chastised Prahlāda as follows:

An actual *brāhmaṇa* is satisfied to see everyone as a devotee of Krsna, what to speak of a disciple. But Śaṇḍa and Amarka did not have real brahminical qualifications and served demons.

16-17. They chastised Prahlāda, "Bring a stick. He deserves punishment. By his bad intelligence (*durbuddhi*), he is defaming our dynasty like a cinder (*kulāṅgāra*). He is like a thorn tree in the sandalwood forest of demoniac dynasty. Viṣṇu is like the axe (*paraśu*) to cut that forest and Prahlāda is like the handle of that axe."

18. They forcefully taught Prahlāda the paths of religion, economic development and sense gratification (*dharma, artha* and *kāma*).

19-24: Prahlāda describes nava-vidhā-bhakti to Hiraṇyakaśipu

19. Next meeting: Śaṇḍa and Amarka thought that Prahlāda was educated in the four diplomatic principles[5] (*catuṣṭayaṁ*) of public leaders. One day after Prahlāda was nicely bathed and decorated by his mother, they presented him before his father.

20-21. Fatherly affection: Prahlāda offered obeisances to Hiraṇyakaśipu, who then happily embraced him and showered his blessings. Placing Prahlāda on his lap, Hiraṇyakaśipu spoke with affection and tears in his eyes that moistened the boy.

22. Hiraṇyakaśipu asked Prahlāda: "My dear son, please repeat whatever you think is the best of the knowledge taught by your teacher."

Prahlāda had two kinds of teachers – Śukrācārya's sons who taught him materialistic diplomacy, and Nārada Muni who enlightened him in spiritual knowledge when he was in his mother's womb. The teacher refers to the son of Śukrācārya from Hiraṇyakaśipu's point of view, but it refers to Nārada from Prahlāda's point of view. Thus Prahlāda replies with what he learnt from Nārada Muni.

[5] They are – (*i*) *sāma*, the process of pacifying (*ii*) *dāna*, the process of giving money in charity (*iii*) *bheda*, the principle of dividing and (*iv*) *daṇḍa*, the principle of punishment.

23-24. Prahlāda's reply: "Nine processes of Bhakti"	
śravaṇaṁ kīrtanaṁ viṣṇoḥ	(1) Hearing about the glories of Supreme Lord. Ex: Parīkṣit (2) Chanting Viṣṇu's names, qualities and pastimes. Ex: Śukadeva
smaraṇaṁ pāda-sevanam	(3) Remembering Him. Ex: Prahlāda Mahārāja (4) Serving His lotus feet (menial service). Ex: Lakṣmīdevī
arcanaṁ vandanaṁ dāsyaṁ	(5) Worshiping His deity with 16 types of paraphernalia. Ex: Pṛthu (6) Offering prayers unto Him. Ex: Akrūra (7) Becoming His servant. Ex: Hanumān
sakhyam ātma-nivedanam	(8) Considering Him one's best friend, with firm faith. Ex: Arjuna (9) Surrendering everything unto Him (i.e., serving Him with body, mind and words). Ex: Ambarīṣa Mahārāja
iti puṁsārpitā viṣṇau bhaktiś cen nava-lakṣaṇā	These are nine kinds of devotional service offered by a human being unto the Supreme Lord Viṣṇu or Kṛṣṇa
kriyeta bhagavaty addhā tan manye 'dhītam uttamam	One who has dedicated his life to such service is the most learned, for he has acquired complete knowledge

25-29: Hiraṇyakaśipu's anger

25-27. Hiraṇyakaśipu became angry and chastised the teachers: "O unqualified *brāhmaṇa* (*brahma-bandhu*). You have disobeyed my order and taught this poor boy this nonsense (*asāram*) about devotional service to my enemy! Your real nature is now manifested. The enmity of deceptive friends (like you) in false garbs will be manifest in course of time, just as disease manifests in sinful man."

Asāram means unworthy or insubstantial. For a demon there is no substance in *bhakti*, but to a devotee devotional service is the only essential factor in life.

28. The son of Śukrācārya replied, "We did not teach anything that your son spoke. *Bhakti* has naturally developed in him. Please do not accuse us unnecessarily."

29. Hiraṇyakaśipu asked Prahlāda, "You are most fallen of our family. If your *gurus* haven't taught you this knowledge, where have you gotten this inauspicious mentality (*abhadra-asati-mati*)?"

30-32: Prahlāda instructs bhakti to Hiraṇyakaśipu more strongly

30. Nature and destination of materialistic householders	
matir na kṛṣṇe parataḥ svato vā mitho 'bhipadyeta gṛha-vratānām	The attached householders' inclination towards Kṛṣṇa is never aroused by (*i*) others' instructions (*ii*) own efforts or (*iii*) a combination of both

adānta-gobhir viśatāṁ tamisraṁ	Due to uncontrolled senses, they enter hellish life
punaḥ punaś carvita-carvaṇānām	and repeatedly chew the chewed

Same product, different packaging: As long as one has sex desire, one must transmigrate from one body to another to enjoy sex in different species. Although the forms may differ (demigod, human, animal etc.), the business of sex is the same. Whether we squeeze sugar out of the sugarcane with our teeth or a machine, the result is the same—sugarcane juice.

Understanding Kṛṣṇa is possible only by serving a pure devotee and training under him.

31. Materialists are ignorant, ambitious, misled and entangled	
na te viduḥ svārtha-gatiṁ hi viṣṇuṁ	**Ignorant:** They don't understand that Lord Viṣṇu is their real interest (goal of life)
durāśayā ye bahir-artha-māninaḥ	**Ambitious:** Being ambitious to enjoy material world, they consider sense objects valuable
andhā yathāndhair upanīyamānās	**Misled:** As blind men (bogus *gurus*) led by another blind man fall into ditch
te 'pīśa-tantryām uru-dāmni baddhāḥ	**Entangled:** they are strongly bound by ropes of material nature and suffer threefold miseries

32. Power of serving a Vaiṣṇava	
naiṣāṁ matis tāvad urukramāṅghriṁ spṛśaty anarthāpagamo yad-arthaḥ	Their consciousness will not be attached to Lord Urukrama's lotus feet that destroys unwanted things (*samsāra*)
mahīyasāṁ pāda-rajo-'bhiṣekaṁ niṣkiñcanānāṁ na vṛṇīta yāvat	till they smear their bodies with the dust of great devotees, who are free from material contamination

33-44: Hiraṇyakaśipu's Attempts to Kill Prahlāda

33-34b. Hiraṇyakaśipu, blinded by anger, threw Prahlāda off his lap and onto the ground. Indignant and angry, his eyes were reddish like molten copper.

Although Prahlāda maintained an attitude of noncooperation with the philosophy of his father, yet he was tolerant and humble. But Hiraṇyakaśipu, being a nondevotee, wanted to kill his own small son.

34b-36. Hiraṇyakaśipu ordered his servants to kill Prahlāda: "O demons! This boy deserves to be killed. Kill him as soon as possible! He is the killer of my brother, for he

is engaged in *bhakti* of our enemy Viṣṇu. Even at this young age he has given up his affection for his parents. He is certainly untrustworthy."

Prahlāda would be elevated to *sārūpya* liberation (that awards one to have a similar form as Lord Viṣṇu) and in that sense he resembled Lord Viṣṇu.

34b-36. Hiraṇyakaśipu ordered his servants to kill Prahlāda: "O demons! This boy deserves to be killed. Kill him as soon as possible! He is the killer of my brother, for he is engaged in *bhakti* of our enemy Viṣṇu. Even at this young age he has given up his affection for his parents. He is certainly untrustworthy."

Hiraṇyakaśipu's servants might ask him, "How can *we* kill *your* son?"

37-38. Hiraṇyakaśipu justifies killing his son

- **"Medicinal herb**, though born in the forest, if beneficial, must be kept carefully. Similarly, if an outsider is favorable, he must be protected like a son.
- **A bodily limb** must be amputated, if it is diseased, so that the rest of the body may live happily. Similarly, even one's own son, if unfavorable, must be rejected.

- **Uncontrolled senses** are the enemies of all *yogīs*. Similarly, this Prahlāda is an enemy because I cannot control him. So he must be killed by all means."

39-44: Attempts to kill Prahlāda fail

39-41. Prahlāda's undisturbed meditation: The fierce looking demons then began striking the tender parts of Prahlāda with their tridents. But Prahlāda sat silently meditating on Viṣṇu, the unchangeable, transcendental Supersoul of the entire universe. The demons' weapons had no tangible effects on Prahlāda, like the good deeds of an unfortunate person.

42. Hiraṇyakaśipu became fearful and began contriving other means to kill Prahlāda.

43-44. Various attempts to kill Prahlāda: Hiraṇyakaśipu couldn't kill Prahlāda by –

i. Throwing him beneath the feet of big elephants
ii. Throwing him among huge snakes
iii. Employing destructive spells
iv. Hurling him from the top of a hill

v. Conjuring up illusory tricks
vi. Imprisoning him
vii. Administering poison
viii. Starving him
ix. Exposing him to severe cold, winds, fire and water
x. Throwing heavy stones to crush him

When all these failed, Hiraṇyakaśipu was in great anxiety about what to do next.

45-57: Prahlāda Sent to School Again

45-47. Hiraṇyakaśipu's thoughts, "I called him many ill names and devised many means to kill him, but he saved himself by his own powers. Although near to me and merely a child, he is completely fearless, never forgetting Viṣṇu. He is like a dog's tail (*śunaḥ-śepa*), never to be straightened. His strength is unlimited. He appears immortal. Perhaps due to my enmity toward him, I shall die."

48-50. Śaṇḍa and Amarka advised Hiraṇyakaśipu secretly, "There is no reason for you to be morose. You have conquered all three worlds. All the demigods are afraid simply by the movement of your eyebrows. Prahlāda is a small child and his bad or good qualities have no value. Until Śukrācārya returns, arrest him with Varuṇa's ropes, so that he will not flee in fear. He will change by age and service to *ācārya*."

51. Hiraṇyakaśipu agreed to their instructions and requested them to instruct royal household duties (*rājñāṁ yo gṛha-medhinām*) to Prahlāda.

52. Śaṇḍa and Amarka taught Prahlāda, who was very submissive and humble, about *dharma*, *artha* and *kāma* very systematically and unceasingly.

53. Prahlāda did not like them, for such instructions are based on the duality of worldly affairs, which involve one in a materialistic way of life.

54. Prahlāda's classmates would call him for playing, in the absence of teachers.

55. Prahlāda addressed his friends in sweet words (*ślakṣṇayā vācā*) and began to teach them about the uselessness of the materialistic way of life.

56-57. All the children were – (*i*) respectful (*gauravāt*) to Prahlāda, and (*ii*) not so polluted (*adūṣita-dhiyo*) by their teachers. So they surrounded Prahlāda to hear him with eyes fixed on him. Prahlāda, a *mahā-bhāgavata*, desired their welfare and began instructing them.

7.6 Prahlāda Instructs His Demoniac Schoolmates

1-5: Right utility of human life

- 1-2: A human being should practice bhakti right from one's childhood.
- 3-5: Instead of endeavouring for happiness of the senses that is automatically obtained, one should endeavour for the highest goal.

6-18: How is human life misused?

- 6-8: 100 years of human life – 50 years in sleep, 20 years in childhood, 20 years in oldage and the rest in family attachments.
- 9-10: Strong attachment in materialistic household life
- 11-15: Insatiable family attachments and absorption in family maintenance
- 16-18: Even the wise are entangled; Liberation is rare; Solution is to take shelter of Lord Nārāyaṇa

19-26: Instructions on worshiping the Supreme Lord

- 19-24: Pleasing the all-pervading Supreme Lord is not very difficult. One has to be merciful to all.
- 25-26: Nothing is unobtainable when Viṣṇu is satisfied. Therefore, surrender unto Him.

27-30: Prahlāda concludes and his classmates inquire from him

- Prahlāda told he received this knowledge from Nārada Muni. His classmates asked him how did he hear from Nārada Muni.

Prahlāda Mahārāja instructs his schoolmates about *bhakti* in their leisure time.

1-5: Right Utility of Human Life

1. Human life is very rare	
kaumāra ācaret prājño	Right from one's childhood, an intelligent person
dharmān bhāgavatān iha	should perform devotional service in this life.
durlabhaṁ mānuṣaṁ janma	Because the human form of life is rarely achieved.
tad apy adhruvam arthadam	Although temporary it is very effective for *bhakti*.

The normal progression of ages is *kaumāra* from 1-5 years, *paugaṇḍa* from 5-10 years, *kaiśora* from 10-15 years and *yauvana* above 15 years.

Why bhakti from kaumāra age? – One may say that one can start *bhakti* in *yauvana* also! But the wise person understands that he may die at the end of *kaumāra* age. One may say that one can practice *bhakti* in a future life as well! Human birth is very rare. Although human life is also short, it is effective (*arthadam*). King Khātvāṅga and others achieved success by having *bhakti* for only a few moments.

How to perform *bhāgavata-dharma*? One should perform it by the methods which enable one to attain surrender to the lotus feet of Lord Viṣṇu.

2. Every human being must do devotional service to the lotus feet of Lord Viṣṇu (*viṣṇoḥ pādopasarpaṇam*). This is natural because Viṣṇu is the most beloved (*priya*), the master of the soul (*ātmeśvaraḥ*), and the well-wisher (*suhṛt*) of all beings.

Goal of education: The *jīva* has an eternal intimate relation with the Supreme Lord. But because he has forgotten it, he is suffering, life after life. Our eternal relationship with God can be revived in the human life, and that should be the goal of education.

What is the problem with endeavoring for material happiness?

3. Happiness of the senses can be obtained –

i. due to possessing a material body (*deha yogena*)
ii. in any species (*sarvatra labhyate*)
iii. without endeavour (*ayatnataḥ*)
iv. by superior arrangement (*daivād*)

just as one obtains distress without endeavor.

sukham aindriyakaṁ daityā deha-yogena dehinām
sarvatra labhyate daivād yathā duḥkham ayatnataḥ

Best utility of human life lies in reviving our relation with God, instead of wasting one's time and energy to fight against distress and work hard for happiness.

4. One shouldn't endeavor for material happiness, for it only depletes one's lifespan (*āyur-vyayaḥ*), and results in no benefit (*na tathā vindate kṣemaṁ*). One must endeavor for worshiping the lotus feet of Lord Mukunda to surely attain the spiritual platform.

tat-prayāso na kartavyo yata āyur-vyayaḥ param
na tathā vindate kṣemaṁ mukunda-caraṇāmbujam

5. Conclusion: Therefore, while in material existence (*bhavam āśritaḥ*), an intelligent human being must endeavor for the highest goal of life as long as the body is strong.

Bhavam āśritaḥ refers to unnecessary problems in this world. This can also be read as *bhayam āśritah*, which means material life is full of anxiety and fear.

Prahlāda's instruction in Verse 2 indicates *rāga-bhakti* or spontaneous devotional service and Verse 5 indicates *vaidhi-bhakti* or regulated devotional service.

6-18: How Is Human Life Misused?

6-8. The 100 years of human life are wasted by one whose senses are uncontrolled –

- 50 years in sleep (12 hours of daily sleep)
- 20 years in childhood and sporting
- 20 years in oldage / invalidity
- Remaining years in family attachments

Thus one wastes one's human life without taking interest in devotional service.

Thus at the time of death, one is transferred into another material body. Therefore a life of lusty desires and sense gratification is extremely risky.

9-18: Entangling materialistic family affairs

9. An attached householder with uncontrolled senses (*ajitendriyaḥ*), is bound strongly by ropes of affection (*sneha-pāśair dṛḍhair baddham*) for his family and cannot be liberated.

Even if one realizes that he should worship Kṛṣṇa, he is unable to do so. Therefore from the *kaumāra* age one should begin worshipping the Lord. One can perfect one's worship only by attachment to worship and detachment towards other things.

Training as a *brahmacārī* in the beginning of one's life enables one to lead a proper *gṛhastha* or householder life and progress towards spiritual realization.

10. Strength of material attachment: Who can give up desire for money (*artha-tṛṣṇāṁ*), which is dearer than one's life? Thieves, servants and merchants try to get money even by risking their lives.

11-13. Insatiable family attachments

- **Wife** is kind and sympathetic and pleases her husband in a solitary place
- **Children** talk sweet words, in broken language, which is pleasing to hear
- **Parents** and one's children are very dear
- **Daughter** is especially dear to her father, and is always in his mind.
- **Household** furniture, domestic animals and servants give comfort.
- **Genitals** and **tongue** bind one by material conditions

Unable to give up attachment to these things, the foolish householder, acting out of lust with unsatisfied desires (*lobha, avitṛpta kāma*), perishes. He is just like a silkworm that is imprisoned in its own cocoon, with no way to escape.

14-15. Absorption in family maintenance (*kuṭumba-poṣa, kutumba-rāmaḥ*) leads to –

i. exhaustion of lifespan
ii. defeat of the real purpose of human life (*atha vihatam*)
iii. no regret or distaste for enjoyment despite sufferings in material existence
iv. no sense control (*ajitendriya*)
v. unfulfilled desires (*aśānta kāma*)
vi. obsessed with accumulating money, even by stealing or cheating, despite knowing that one will be punished now (by government) and after death (by Yamarāja).

Prahlāda Mahārāja has described earlier that the increasingly entangling family life centered around sex life is like a dark well (See 7.5.5 and 7.9.45) and that one should give it up to take shelter of the Supreme Lord.

16. Even the learned (*vidvān*) are overcome by ignorance like a fool (*vimūḍha*) and get absorbed in family affairs, incapable of understanding oneself and get bewildered by the separatist conceptions of 'self and others' (*svīya-pārakya-vibhinna-bhāva*).

17. Rarity of liberation: No one bereft of knowledge of the Supreme Lord has been able to liberate oneself from material bondage at any time or anywhere. Addicted to sense gratification, the demons become playthings in the hands of women (*krīḍā-mṛga*) and are shackled in the expansions of family relationships.

Then what is the solution to come out of this family entanglement?

18. Solution: Although you are sons of demons, (*i*) keep aloof from the association of demons and (*ii*) take shelter of Lord Nārāyaṇa, the origin of all demigods. Because the ultimate goal for the devotees is liberation from material bondage.

19-26: Instructions On Worshiping the Supreme Lord

19-24: Pleasing the Supreme Lord

19. Pleasing Lord Nārāyaṇa takes no great endeavor as He is the Supersoul in all beings, and father of all. There is no impediment in worshiping Him in all directions, in all times and from all angles of vision.

na hy acyutaṁ prīṇayato bahv-āyāso 'surātmajāḥ
ātmatvāt sarva-bhūtānāṁ siddhatvād iha sarvataḥ

One's duty is to revive one's relationship with Nārāyaṇa by *bhakti* that constitutes *śravaṇaṁ kīrtanaṁ* etc. (See 7.5.23). A slight endeavor in this direction will make the attempt successful, whereas one will never be successful in pleasing his so-called family, society and nation, even if one endeavors to sacrifice his life.

Prahlāda's friends, who were born of demon families, thought that realizing the Supreme Lord was difficult. But the Lord is most intimately related to all *jīvas* and is present everywhere. Therefore if one understands this Vaiṣṇava philosophy, realize Him is not at all difficult.

20-21. The infallible Supreme Lord is present everywhere – in all higher and lower beings from Brahmā to non-moving beings, in all material elements, in the *mahat-tattva* (total material energy), in the three modes, in the unmanifested material nature and the false ego. Although He is one, He is all-pervading.

22-23. Other qualities of the Lord: He is the all-pervading Supersoul, cause of all causes, observer in the hearts of all living entities, changeless and undivided. He is perceived as the supreme *sac-cid-ānanda* [eternity, knowledge and bliss]. Being covered by the curtain of *māyā*, He appears non-existent to the atheist.

When *māyā* is overcome by *bhakti* to the Supreme Lord, the Lord becomes visible according to the degree of *bhakti*.

Since the Lord can be realized by *bhakti*, *bhakti* should be made steady, without obstacles, by showing mercy and friendship to all beings.

24. Pleasing the Lord by being merciful to all	
tasmāt sarveṣu bhūteṣu dayāṁ kuruta sauhṛdam	Therefore show compassion and affection to all living beings and be their well-wishers.
bhāvam āsuram unmucya	And please give up your demoniac nature.
yayā tuṣyaty adhokṣajaḥ	Thus the Supreme Lord will be satisfied.

People are generally ignorant of Kṛṣṇa consciousness, and therefore to become their best well-wisher one should teach them about Kṛṣṇa consciousness without discrimination.

And that service pleases the Supreme Lord the most. Prahlāda thinks, "If Bhakti-devi, by the mercy of *guru* and Vaiṣṇavas, accepts me, then the Lord will also be directly visible."

If the Lord is satisfied, what is use of other goals of aspiration? The devotees are like bees, who by their nature do not desire other things.

25-26: Surrendering unto the Lord and its result

25. Nothing is unobtainable if the Lord is satisfied. He is unlimited and the cause of all causes. Since the devotees glorify the lotus feet of the Lord, for them, what is the use of *dharma, artha, kāma* and *mokṣa,* which are all automatically obtainable under the influence of material modes?

Hearing this from Prahlāda, his schoolmates might ask, "If *dharma*, *artha* and *kāma* are not the goals of human life, why have the two sons of Śukrācarya said these are prescribed in the Vedas?" Prahlāda says, "I do not criticize them, since they are approved for some persons. What is actually beneficial for the saintly (*satyam*) is surrender to the Supreme Lord."

26. Surrender to Viṣṇu's lotus feet is transcendental. I consider the other process within the *tri-vargas* (*dharma, artha* and *kāma*), namely education, rituals, logic, law and order and means of earning livelihood etc., to be external and material.

To give the boys faith, Prahlāda explains the *guru sampradāya.*

27-30: Prahlāda Concludes and His Classmates Inquire From Him

27. Lord Nārāyaṇa gave this pure knowledge (*jñānaṁ amalaṁ*) to Nārada Muni earlier. This can be understood by fully surrendered devotees (*ekāntināṁ*) with no material desires (*akiñcanānāṁ*), who bathe their bodies in the dust from the Lord's lotus feet (*pādāravinda-rajasāpluta-dehināṁ*). They understand this in *paramparā.*

28. I received this knowledge of *bhāgavata-dharma* from Nārada Muni. This is fully scientific and based on logic and philosophy, and is free from material contamination.

29-30. Prahlāda's schoolmates asked him, "We have only Śaṇḍa and Amarka, as our teachers. We are dependent on them and especially you always live with in palace! How then did you hear from Nārada Muni?"

7.7 What Prahlāda Learned in the Womb

- **1-17:** Events leading to Kayādhu's stay at Nārada Muni's āśrama
  - 1-7: When Hiraṇyakaśipu was doing austerities, the demigods attacked the demons and arrested Kayādhu
  - 9-11: Nārada Muni stopped the demigods and said that the child in Kayādhu's womb would be a great devotee
  - 12-17: Merciful Nārada brought Kayādhu to his āśrama and spoke transcendental knowledge to the mother and the child in her womb
- **18-28:** Jñāna – Knowledge of spirit soul and transmigration
  - 18-24: The nature of the spirit soul
  - 25-28: Destroying the polluted material intelligence by Kṛṣṇa consciousness
- **29-38:** Prahlāda's instructions on bhakti
  - 29-32: The activities and results of bhakti, the best of all paths
  - 33-38: Advanced stages of bhakti
- **39-47:** Struggle for material things is unworthy
  - 39-42: The transient nature of material happiness
  - 43-47: The material body, its possessions and relations
- **48-55:** Prahlāda urges his schoolmates to take to bhakti
  - 48-52: Depending on the Supreme Lord Mukunda and pleasing Him by service is most auspicious
  - 53-55: Therefore, everyone should take to kṛṣṇa-bhakti, the ultimate goal of human life

To answer his schoolmates, Prahlāda relates how he had acquired spiritual knowledge from Nārada Muni when he was in the womb of his mother.

1-17: Events Leading to Kayādhu's Stay at Nārada Muni's Āśrama

1. Prahlāda remembered the words of Nārada Muni and spoke to his friends as follows:

2-5. The demigods attack the demons: When my father Hiraṇyakaśipu went to perform austerities, the demigods attacked the demons thinking, "Hiraṇyakaśipu is now defeated by his own sinful reactions just as a serpent is eaten by small ants." Seeing the demigods killing the leaders of the demons, other demons left their homes and relatives and fled to protect their lives.

6-7. Indra arrests Kayādhu: The demigods plundered Hiraṇyakaśipu's palace and Indra arrested his queen Kayādhu. When she was being led away, crying like a *kurarī* bird captured by a vulture, Nārada Muni appeared there and saw her.

8. Nārada stops Indra, "This woman is sinless and chaste wife of another man. You should not drag her off in this merciless way. Release her immediately."

9. Indra told his plan to Nārada, "She is carrying the seed of the great demon. Let her remain in our custody until her child is delivered, and then we shall release her."

Indra's plan was to kill the child as soon as he was born. He expected the child to be another great demon like his father Hiraṇyakaśipu.

10-11. Nārada said about the child, "The child in her womb is sinless (*niṣkilbiṣaḥ*), a great devotee (*mahā-bhāgavata*) and a powerful servant of Lord Viṣṇu. You will not be able to kill him." Hearing this, the demigods released my mother and circumambulated her (to offer respects to the devotee within her womb).

Obedience to paramparā: Although the demigods are exalted, they were obedient to Nārada Muni and accepted his authoritative statements. This is called understanding by the *paramparā* system. There is no need to speculate about God and His devotee. One should just accept the statements of a bona fide devotee.

12-14. Later Nārada Muni brought her to his āśrama and told her to remain there until her husband comes back from his asuterities. Thus my mother stayed there under Nārada Muni's care without fear. She desired to give birth after the arrival of her husband. At the *āśrama* she rendered service unto Nārada Muni with great devotion.

15. Merciful Nārada instructed both the mother and the child in her womb. These instructions on religion and transcendental knowledge (*dharmasya tattvaṁ jñānaṁ ca*) were free from all material contamination (*nirmalam*).

The words '*nirmalam*' '*dharma*,' refer to spotless religion i.e., *bhāgavata-dharma* or pure *bhakti-yoga*. Ordinary ritualistic activities constitute contaminated religion.

Prahlāda's schoolmates might ask him, "But why don't we see *bhakti* in your mother?"

16. The mother forgot the instructions because of the long duration of time that has passed and because of her being a woman; but due to the blessings of Nārada Muni, I could not forget them.

Prahlāda's mother was more concerned with protecting the child in the womb and was very anxious to see her husband return. Therefore she could not consider very seriously the sublime instructions of Nārada Muni.

17. If you put faith in my words, you can also understand spiritual knowledge like me, although you are children. Women also can understand.

One cannot imagine how a baby in embryo could hear Nārada Muni. But progress in spiritual life and reception of spiritual knowledge cannot be obstructed by any material condition. This is called *ahaituky apratihatā*. Prahlāda's speaking of spiritual knowledge to his classmates was also certainly effective, although all of them were children.

18-28: Jñāna – Knowledge of Spirit Soul and Transmigration

18-24: The nature of the spirit soul

18. Soul doesn't undergo any changes but the body undergoes six changes, namely birth, existence, growth, transformation, dwindling and death, just as fruits and flowers of tree undergo changes.

19-20. Twelve qualities of ātmā (Supersoul or soul)

i. Eternal, without birth or death (*nitya*)
ii. Free from deterioration (*avyaya*)
iii. Pure, without material contamination (*śuddha*)
iv. Individual (*eka*)
v. Knower of body (*kṣetra-jña*)
vi. Shelter of everything (*āśraya*)
vii. Free from material change (*avikriya*)
viii. Self-illuminated (*sva-dṛk*)
ix. Cause of all causes (*hetu*)
x. All-pervading/ spreading throughout body as consciousness (*vyāpaka*)
xi. Independent of material body (*asaṅgī*)
xii. Always uncovered (*anāvṛtaḥ*)

With these transcendental qualities, a learned person must give up the false conception (*asat-bhāvam*) of 'I and mine' (*aham-mama*), born of illusion (*moha-jam*).

Who can know the existence of the spirit within the body?

21. Understanding spirit: Just as an expert geologist can extract gold from gold ore, a spiritually advanced person (*adhyātma-vit*) can attain perfection in spiritual life and understand the soul and Supersoul within the body by spiritual processes (*ātma-yogaiḥ*).

The above verse spoke about knower of *ādhyātma*. The next verse says what is *adhyātma*.

22. The soul exists as observer within the 8 energies, 3 modes and 16 transformations.

The 8 external energies are *prakṛti*, *mahat-tattva*, false ego and the five sense objects.
The 3 modes of material nature are goodness, passion and ignorance.
The 16 transformations are the eleven senses and five gross elements (earth, water etc).

23. The two kinds of bodies of the individual soul are – (*i*) a gross body made of five gross elements and (*ii*) a subtle body made of three subtle elements. By analysis, one must separate spirit from matter.

24. A sober person must search for the soul with mind purified through analytical study of the soul's connection with (*anvaya*) and distinction from (*vyatireka*) all things that undergo creation, maintenance and destruction.

25-28: Destroying the polluted material intelligence

25. Intelligence has three states of activity—wakefulness (*jāgaraṇaṁ*), dreaming (*svapna*) and deep sleep (*suṣupti*). The person who perceives all these three states is the original master, Paramātmā, the Supreme Personality of Godhead.

He who activates that material intelligence is the Paramātmā. He who is endowed with the intelligence is the *jīva*, who is beyond the various states of intelligence.

26. One can understand the pure soul by rejecting these three states of intelligence composed of the three material modes, just as one can understand the presence of the air by the aromas it carries.

The soul is only the observer of the three states of intelligence. The activities of the body are not the activities of the soul, just as aromas are distinct from air, the material vehicle in which they are carried.

27. Polluted intelligence entangles the *jīva* in material life and three modes. Its root is not understood (*ajñāna-mūlaḥ*). Though insubstantial (*apārthaḥ*), it imposes the body on the *jīva* (*saṁsāra*), just as a dream is imposed on a person.

One can destroy this polluted intelligence by devotional service unto Lord Kṛṣṇa.

28. Destroy this material intelligence by Kṛṣṇa consciousness that can – (*i*) burn the seed of fruitive activities, (*ii*) stop the flow of the intelligence in three states and (*iii*) dissipate the ignorance.

Having described the nature of spirit soul and its entanglement in material existence due to the gross and subtle bodies, Prahlāda will now describe in detail the process of coming out of this entanglement – i.e., devotional service unto the Supreme Lord Kṛṣṇa.

29-38: Prahlāda's Instructions On Bhakti

29-33: The activities and results of bhakti

29. Bhakti is the best of all paths recommended for disentanglement from matter. It is directly spoken by the Supreme Lord and is the easiest way of developing love of God.

tatropāya-sahasrāṇām ayaṁ bhagavatoditaḥ
yad īśvare bhagavati yathā yair añjasā ratiḥ

30-32. Various activities of bhakti		
i	*guru-śuśrūṣayā bhaktyā*	Serving a bona fide *guru* with faith and devotion.
ii	*sarva-labdhārpaṇena ca*	Offer all one's possession to *guru* or Kṛṣṇa.
iii	*saṅgena sādhu-bhaktānām*	Associating with saintly persons and devotees.
iv	*īśvarārādhanena ca*	Worshiping the Supreme Lord.
v	*śraddhayā tat-kathāyāṁ ca*	Hearing the glories of the Lord with faith.
vi	*kīrtanair guṇa-karmaṇām*	Glorifying the Lord's divine qualities and activities.
vii	*tat-pādāmburuha-dhyānāt*	Always meditating on the Lord's lotus feet.
viii	*tal-liṅgekṣārhaṇādibhiḥ*	Worshiping the Lord's Deity according to the injunctions of the śāstra and guru.
ix	*hariḥ sarveṣu bhūteṣu bhagavān āsta īśvaraḥ*	Remember the Lord as the Paramātmā situated in the core of every living entity's heart.
x	*iti bhūtāni manasā kāmais taiḥ sādhu mānayet*	Respecting all living entities according to their position or manifestation.

By performing the above activities of *bhakti* one can attain the following results.

33. Results of bhakti activities

i. **Secondary result:** One can cut down the influence of lust, anger, greed, illusion, madness and jealousy (*nirjita-ṣaḍ-vargaiḥ*).

ii. **Primary result:** One attains the platform of *rati* or loving service to Lord Vāsudeva (*saṁlabhyate ratiḥ*).

The next verse describes the symptoms of *rati.*

34-38: Advanced stages of bhakti

34-35. Symptoms of rati: Upon hearing about the incomparable (*atulyān*) qualities and pastimes of the Lord, the devotee becomes choked up, his hairs stand on end, his voice falters, his eyes shed tears, and he sings, shouts and dances. As if haunted by a ghost (*graha-grasta*), he laughs and cries. He meditates, contemplates, offers respects to all, breathes heavily, gives up shame and shouts like a madman, "Hare Kṛṣṇa! O Nārāyaṇa! O master of the universe!"

36. Attaining particular bhāva: By constantly thinking of the Lord, the devotee is freed from all material bondage (*mukta-samasta-bandhana*). The seeds of his material desires are burnt to ashes (*nirdagdha-bījānuśayo*). By such *bhakti* (*rāga-bhakti*) one achieves the shelter of the Lord and directly contacts Him.

37. Direct contact with the Lord by *bhakti* destroys the cycle of *saṁsāra* (repeated birth and death) for the embodied souls. Therefore worship the Lord in your heart.

38. Worshiping the Lord is easy. He is in everyone's heart, and is the friend of all *jīvas*. What, then, is the need for unnecessary endeavour for sense gratification?

Having emphasized the glory of performing devotional service unto the Supreme Lord, Prahlāda will now describe the worthlessness of material pursuits, that act as obstacles in *bhakti.*

39-47: Struggle for Material Things Is Unworthy

39-42: The transient nature of material happiness

39. Material opulence is temporary. How much pleasure can ephemeral riches, wife, animals, children, residence and other luxuries offer to a human being with life span that is perishable in a moment (*kṣaṇa-bhaṅgura āyuṣaḥ*)?

rāyaḥ kalatraṁ paśavaḥ sutādayo
gṛhā mahī kuñjara-kośa-bhūtayaḥ
sarve 'rtha-kāmāḥ kṣaṇa-bhaṅgurāyuṣaḥ
kurvanti martyasya kiyat priyaṁ calāḥ

40a. Even heaven is temporary. By sacrifices one may be elevated to heavenly planets, but they are also impure and not free from the taint of material existence.

40b. So, worship the Supreme Lord with great devotion for your own benefit and self-realization. He is free from all inebrieties.

41. A materialist (karmī) is frustrated in his attempts to attain better enjoyment. Although he thinks of himself highly learned, he inevitably gets opposite results.

How then are the materialists happy sometimes?

42. The happiness and distress of karmīs	
sukhāya duḥkha-mokṣāya saṅkalpa iha karmiṇaḥ	In this world, every materialist desires and acts to achieve happiness and diminish distress.
sadāpnotīhayā duḥkham	But they achieve only unhappiness by their actions.
anīhāyāḥ sukhāvṛtaḥ	By giving up desire for enjoyment, they get happiness.

One is happy as long as one does not endeavor for happiness; as soon as one begins his activities for happiness, his conditions of distress begin.

43-47: The material body, its possessions and relations

43. Comfort seeking body: A living entity desires and acts for comfort of one's body. But the perishable body, which is property of others, embraces the *jīva* and leaves him aside.

kāmān kāmayate kāmyair yad-artham iha pūruṣaḥ
sa vai dehas tu pārakyo bhaṅguro yāty upaiti ca

The material body is meant to be eaten by dogs, jackals or moths and thus turned into useless stool, ashes or earth. The living entity wastes his time in a futile attempt to gain material possessions for the comfort of one body after another.

44. False bodily possessions: As the body itself is meant to become stool or earth, there is no meaning to the paraphernalia related to the body, such as wife, children, servants, residences and so on.

45. Perishable bodily relations: Relation with this paraphernalia is finished when the body is finished. For a devotee who experiences an ocean of eternal bliss in worshiping the Lord (*nityānanda-rasodadheḥ*), bodily relations are most insignificant.

46. Karma causes bodies: The living entity receives different material bodies due to one's previous fruitive activities (*karma*) and thus suffers. Knowing this, who will be interested in fruitive acts that result in miseries?

47. Cycle of transmigration: The *jīva* receives one type of body as per his *karma* and by performing actions with that body he creates another body. Thus one continues in the cycle of birth and death.

48-55: Prahlāda Urges His Schoolmates to Take to Bhakti

48. Depend on the Supreme Lord with devotion and without material desires (*anīha*). He is the shelter of *dharma, artha* and *kāma.*

49. Lord Hari is the Supersoul (*ātma*) of all *jīvas.* Every one is manifestation of His energy. He is the supreme controller (*īśvara*) and most dear (*priya*) to all.

50. Most auspicious condition of life (*svastimān*) is to be situated in the service of Lord Mukunda (*bhajan mukunda-caraṇaṁ*) like me (Prahlāda). This can be done by anyone including demigods, demons, humans, Yakṣas, Gandharvas and so on.

Without *bhakti,* everything else is mockery.

51-52. One cannot please Lord Mukunda by being a *brāhmaṇa*, demigod, sage, or by good conduct, learning, charity, austerity, sacrifice, cleanliness or vows. He is pleased only by unflinching, unalloyed, sincere devotion to Him (*amalayā bhaktyā*).

nālaṁ dvijatvaṁ devatvam ṛṣitvaṁ vāsurātmajāḥ
prīṇanāya mukundasya na vṛttaṁ na bahu-jñatā
na dānaṁ na tapo nejyā na śaucaṁ na vratāni ca
prīyate 'malayā bhaktyā harir anyad viḍambanam

53. Therefore take to bhakti to satisfy the Supreme Lord, the Supersoul of all (*sarva-bhūtātmanīśvare*), in the same favorable way as one takes care of oneself (*ātmaupamyena*).

Bhakti does not depend on good birth.

54. Everyone can perform bhakti. The Yakṣas, Rākṣasas, women, *śūdras,* cowherd men, birds, animals and sinful living entities can revive their original, eternal spiritual existence by accepting the principles of *bhakti-yoga.*

55. The ultimate goal of human life as explained by all the scriptures is to – (*i*) render service to the lotus feet of Govinda, and (*ii*) to see Him everywhere.

etāvān eva loke 'smin puṁsaḥ svārthaḥ paraḥ smṛtaḥ
ekānta-bhaktir govinde yat sarvatra tad-īkṣaṇam

7.8 Lord Nṛsiṁha-deva Slays the King of Demons

1-13: Conversation between Prahlāda and Hiraṇyakaśipu	1-6: Prahlāda's classmates became fixed up in bhakti-yoga. Hiraṇyakaśipu rebuked Prahlāda and asked the source of his strength.
	7-10: Prahlāda says that the Lord is the source of everyone's strength, and advises his father to give up demoniac mentality
	11-13: Hiraṇyakaśipu threatens to kill Prahlāda
14-22: Appearance of Lord Nṛsiṁhadeva	14-17: Hiraṇyakaśipu strikes his fist against the pillar and the Lord appears in a half-man half-lion incarnation to prove the words of His devotee(s) true
	18-22: Astonished, Hiraṇyakaśipu examines the fearsome features of Lord Nṛsiṁhadeva
23-33: Lord Nṛsiṁhadeva kills Hiraṇyakaśipu and the demons	23-28: The fight between Nṛsiṁhadeva and Hiraṇyakaśipu
	29-33: The all-powerful Lord kills Hiraṇyakaśipu and the demons
34-39: The demigods celebrate Lord Nṛsiṁha's victory	Lord Nṛsiṁhadeva sits on Hiraṇyakaśipu's throne and several demigods arrive there to offer respects and worship
40-56: The demigods offer prayers to Lord Nṛsiṁhadeva	Brahmā, Śiva, Indra, Manus, Gandharvas and several others praise Lord Nṛsiṁhadeva for killing Hiraṇyakaśipu and protecting them

Prahlāda's instructions to his schoolmates about *bhakti* became effective and they rejected their teachers Śaṇḍa and Amarka. Hiraṇyakaśipu becomes angry at Prahlāda.

1-13: Conversation Between Prahlāda and Hiraṇyakaśipu

1-6: Prahlāda's effective preaching and Hiraṇyakaśipu's anger

1. The sons of the demons appreciated and accepted Prahlāda's instructions seriously, and rejected the instructions (on diplomacy, politics etc) of their so-called teachers Śaṇḍa and Amarka.

Effective preaching: When a pure devotee (Prahlāda) preaches the glories of the Lord following the footsteps of another pure devotee (Nārada Muni), his preaching is effective.

2. The teachers saw that the boys were becoming fixed in *bhakti-yoga*, they were afraid and reported to Hiraṇyakaśipu.

By associating with a pure devotee and following his instructions, one becomes fixed in Kṛṣṇa consciousness and is not disturbed by materialistic consciousness.

3-4. Hiraṇyakaśipu became angry and decided to kill Prahlāda. Hissing like a trampled snake, he spoke to Prahlāda who was peaceful, mild and gentle, his senses controlled, stood with folded hands.

When one is impudent toward a highly authorized devotee, one is punished by the laws of nature and loses his life span, blessings and the results of pious activities (See SB 10.4.46).

5-6. Hiraṇyakaśipu rebuked Prahlāda, "O most impudent (*durvinīta*), unintelligent (*mandātman*), disruptor of the family (*kula-bheda-kara*), lowest of men (*adhama*), obstinate (*stabdham*), you have violated my power. Today I shall send you to the abode of Yamarāja (*yama-kṣayam*). When I am angry all the planets tremble. Then by whose power are you so fearless?"

Positive meanings of Hiraṇyakaśipu's abusive words towards Prahlāda

- *Durvinīta* → well-behaved, or merciful towards the rascals.
- *Mandātman* → one who is kind to the unfortunate, as he can't tolerate their suffering.
- *Kula-bheda-kara* → one who brings distinction to the family.
- *Adhama* → Prahlāda, like the Prajāpatis, has great power.
- *Stabdham* → Prahlāda does not consider the demons worthy of worship.
- *Yama-kṣayam* → The abode for *yoga* which enables Prahlāda to survive.

7-10: Prahlāda glorifies the Lord and advises his father

7. The Lord is the source of everyone's strength	
na kevalaṁ me bhavataś ca rājan *sa vai balaṁ balināṁ cāpareṣāṁ*	Dear King, not only the source of my strength, the source of your strength and strength of everyone else who is strong, is the Supreme Lord.
pare 'vare 'mī sthira-jaṅgamā ye *brahmādayo yena vaśaṁ praṇītāḥ*	Whether moving or non-moving, superior or inferior, everyone, including Brahmā, is controlled by His strength.

All the different grades of fire derive heat and light from the sun. Similarly, all *jīvas* are dependent on the Supreme Lord's mercy. One's only duty is understand one's subordinate position and surrender unto the Lord.

8. That Supreme Lord is the supreme controller (*īśvara*), time factor (*kāla*), the power of the senses, mind, body and vital force, the best of all living entities, the master of three modes and the creator, maintainer and destroyer of this cosmic manifestation.

9. Give up your demoniac mentality (*āsuram bhāvam*) of discriminating between enemies and friends. Uncontrolled mind (*ajitād ātmanaḥ*) is the only enemy in world. In platform of equality (*samaṁ*), one can worship the Lord perfectly.

Mind control and bhakti: The only bona fide process for controlling the mind is to fix the mind by service to the Lord. We create enemies and friends according to the dictation of the mind, but actually there are no enemies and friends. To understand this is the preliminary condition for entering into the kingdom of devotional service.

10. Enemies are merely imagined due to ignorance. One will have no enemies if one controls the mind and senses, conquers the six plunderers within (lust, anger, greed, illusion, madness and jealousy) and is equiposed to all living entities.

If good instructions are given to a fool, he does not take advantage of them, but becomes more angry. Prahlāda's authorized instructions were not accepted by Hiraṇyakaśipu, who was interested only in money and women. (*hiraṇya* means gold, and *kaśipu* refers to good bedding.) Thus he responded with anger as follows.

11-13: Śrī Hiraṇyakaśipu threatens to kill Prahlāda

Although Hiraṇyakaśipu was a demon, he is described here by the added word *śrī*. Because he fortunately had a great devotee son as Prahlāda. Thus although he was a demon, he would attain salvation and return home, back to Godhead.

11. Desirous of death in my hands, you are speaking confused words (*viklavāḥ giraḥ*) and boasting as if you were better than me at controlling senses, O fool (*mandātman*)!

12. Where is Your Lord? O unfortunate Prahlāda, you always described a Supreme Being who is above everything, controller of everyone, and all-pervading. If He is everywhere, then why is He not present before me in this pillar?

Hiraṇyakaśipu thought himself fortunate as he possessed the property of universe. He called Prahlāda 'unfortunate' because although, as his legitimate son, Prahlāda was to inherit this property, because of his impudence, he was going to die at his father's hands.

In all circumstances a devotee can see the Lord everywhere, whereas the nondevotee can't.

13. I shall now sever your head. Let me see, how your most worshipable God come to protect you.

14-22: Appearance of Lord Nṛsiṁha-deva

14. Striking the pillar: Hiraṇyakaśipu then took up his sword, got up from his royal throne and obsessed with anger he struck his fist against the column.

15-16. From the pillar came a fearful sound, which appeared to crack the covering of the universe. It reached even Brahmaloka and the demigods thought, "Oh, now our planets are being destroyed!" Hiraṇyakaśipu heard that sound, that had never been heard before. Other leaders of the demons were afraid and no one could find its origin.

17. The Lord proves His devotees' words true	
satyaṁ vidhātuṁ nija-bhṛtya-bhāṣitaṁ	To prove that the statement of His servant Prahlāda true
vyāptiṁ ca bhūteṣv akhileṣu cātmanaḥ	that the Lord is present everywhere, in all living entities and elements,
adṛśyatātyadbhuta-rūpam udvahan	Lord Hari appeared in a most wonderful form that was never seen before,
stambhe sabhāyāṁ na mṛgaṁ na mānuṣam	from the pillar in the assembly. That form was neither that of a man nor that of a lion.

Lord Kṛṣṇa told Arjuna to declare that His devotee never perishes (BG 9.31). The Lord preserves the words of His devotees and He appeared as Nara-siṁha, in a half-man half-lion form to make the words of the following devotees true:

Prahlāda had said that the Lord was present everywhere, even in the pillar.

Hiraṇyakaśipu (formerly Jaya, the doorkeeper of Lord Viṣṇu in Vaikuṇṭha) had prayed not to die from created being, inside or outside a residence, and not by man or beast (7.3.35-37). Also he thought, "I may die because of my hatred of Prahlāda." (7.5.47)

Brahmā had sanctioned the desires of Hiraṇyakaśipu (7.4.1-2).

Nārada Muni told that the child in Kayadhu's womb cannot be killed. (7.7.10)

18. Hiraṇyakaśipu was astonished to see the Lord emerging from the pillar. He thought, "What is this creature that is half man and half lion?"

Hiraṇyakaśipu never thought that an animal and human being would be combined so that demons like him would be puzzled by such a form. This is the meaning of the Supreme Personality of Godhead's **omnipotence**.

19-22. Fearsome features of Lord Nṛsiṁha: Hiraṇyakaśipu studied the Lord's form –

- Angry eyes resembling molten gold
- Shining mane, which expanded the dimensions of His fearful face
- Deadly teeth and Razor-sharp tongue, which moved about like a dueling sword
- Ears erect and motionless
- Nostrils and gaping mouth that appeared like mountain caves
- Parted jaws, thick and short neck, broad chest, thin waist
- Entire body touching the sky
- Bodily hairs as white as the rays of the moon
- Arms like flanks of soldiers, spread in all directions killing the demons

23-33: Lord Nṛsiṁha-deva Kills Hiraṇyakaśipu and the Demons

23. Hiraṇyakaśipu attacked Lord Nṛsiṁha with his club thinking, "Lord Viṣṇu has made this plan to kill me, but what is the use? Who can fight with me?"

Lion Vs. elephant: Here Lord Nṛsiṁha appeared like a lion, and Hiraṇyakaśipu attacked Him like an elephant. Therefore this comparison is appropriate, because in the jungle sometimes lions and elephants fight and generally the elephant is defeated by the lion.

24. Hiraṇyakaśipu became invisible within the Lord's effulgence, just as an insect falls into a fire and becomes invisible. This is not astonishing, because the Lord, who is in pure goodness, formerly entered and illuminated the dark universe.

Dissipating darkness: Brahmā saw only darkness in the universe when he was born, but when he received knowledge from the Lord, everything became clear. As long as we are in material modes in this world, we are in darkness. This darkness can only be dissipated by the presence of the Supreme Lord, which is invoked by the practice of *bhakti-yoga*.

Bhakti-yoga: The Lord appeared because of the *bhakti-yoga* of Prahlāda, and as soon as He appeared, the influence of Hiraṇyakaśipu's passion and ignorance was vanquished as the Lord's pure goodness, or the Brahman effulgence.

25-26. The Lord captured Hiraṇyakaśipu along with his club, and then gave him a chance to slip from His hands, just as Garuḍa plays with a snake. But the demigods who were hiding behind the clouds didn't consider it very good.

The demigods knew that if Hiraṇyakaśipu escapes death and sees that the demigods were looking forward for his death, he would take revenge on them. The demigods thought, "Hiraṇyakaśipu has taken our homes. Now, if he lives, he will take our lives!"

27. Hiraṇyakaśipu falsely thought that the Lord was afraid of his prowess. After a while, he again attacked Lord with sword and shield.

28. Laughing loudly the Lord captured Hiraṇyakaśipu. With the speed of a hawk, Hiraṇyakaśipu moved everywhere, but with eyes closed due to fear.

29. Hiraṇyakaśipu's death: Lord Nṛsiṁha captured Hiraṇyakaśipu, just as a snake captures a mouse or Garuḍa captures a snake. The Lord placed the demon on His lap, in the doorway and easily tore him to pieces with His nails, though his body couldn't be pierced by thunderbolt.

To keep the promise of Brahmā intact, Nṛsiṁha-deva killed Hiraṇyakaśipu in this way:

- He pierced him at the door, which was not in the assembly hall, nor outside.
- He placed him on his lap, which which was neither land nor sky.
- He pierced him by his nails, which were neither living nor dead, nor weapons.
- He killed him during the twilight, which was neither day nor night.

30. Lord Nṛsiṁha's condition after killing Hiraṇyakaśipu

- Mouth and mane sprinkled with blood
- Fierce eyes impossible to look at
- Licking the edge of His mouth with His tongue
- Decorated with a garland of the demon's intestines
- Resembled a lion that has just killed an elephant

31. Killing the demons: The Lord uprooted Hiraṇyakaśipu's heart and threw it aside. He then killed the other demons who came to attack, merely with the ends of His nails.

Lord Nṛsiṁha pulled out Hiraṇyakaśipu's heart with His nails as if to inspect it. He thought, "I was living happily in his heart, but how did this unfortunate person make anger and hatred live there as well?"

32-33. The unparalleled prowess of Lord Nṛsiṁha-deva

- His hair on His head – shook the clouds and scattered
- His glaring eyes – stole the effulgence of luminaries
- His breathing – agitated the seas and oceans
- His roaring – made all the elephants to cry in fear
- His hair – threw the airplanes into outer space
- His lotus feet – made earth appear to slip, and all the mountains sprang up
- His effulgence – diminished the natural illumination of the sky and directions

34-39: The Demigods Celebrate Lord Nṛsiṁha's Victory

34. Lord Nṛsiṁha sat on Hiraṇyakaśipu's throne seeing no contestant to face His power. Because of fear and obedience, no one could come forward (i.e., all the demons immediately accepted the Lord's supremacy).

A devotee is always glorious: By sitting on the throne, the Lord showed who should be the king. Although He does not accept the seat offered by sages, purified by *mantras*, He accepted a throne already used and not offered to him, because it belonged to His devotee gatekeeper Jaya, even though he had been cursed and took on the nature of a demon. By this the Lord showed that His devotee is fortunate in any condition of his life.

35. Hiraṇyakaśipu was like fever of meningitis for three worlds. At his death, the wives of the demigods repeatedly showered flowers on Lord Nṛsiṁha, in great joy.

36. The sky was crowded with the airplanes of the demigods, who began beating drums and kettledrums. The heavenly women danced and the Gandharvas sang sweetly.

37-39. All the demigods and sages offered respects to Lord Nṛsiṁha. Brahmā, Śiva, Indra, Pitṛs, Siddhas, Vidyādharas, Nāgas, Gandharvas, Apsaras and many others came.

40-56: The Demigods Offer Prayers to Lord Nṛsiṁha-deva

40. Lord Brahmā: "You possess unlimited potencies that no one can estimate. You easily create, maintain and destroy the universe, yet You remain the same."

41. Lord Śiva: "Your anger is for the end of the universe. As the demon has been killed now, please protect his son Prahlāda Mahārāja, Your surrendered devotee."

42. King Indra: "This demon has taken our shares in sacrifice, which are Yours. He has overtaken our hearts, which are Your residence. Now Your presence dissipated the darkness in our hearts. Your servants do not care even for liberation."

43. The sages: "The process of austerity, with which You create this universe, was stopped by this demon. O protector of the surrendered (*śaraṇya-pāla*), now You have killed him and approved the process of austerity."

44. Pitṛs: "O protector of all religious principles (*akhila-dharma-goptre*), this demon enjoyed all the offerings of *śrāddha* ceremonies done by our descendants. By killing him, You have taken back all this stolen property from his abdomen."

45. Siddhas: "This dishonest demon took our natural mystic powers, and became proud. Now, that he has been killed by Your nails, we offer our obeisances unto You."

46. Vidyādharas: "Proud Hiraṇyakaśipu has banned our power to appear and disappear. Now that he has been killed, we eternally offer obeisances to the pastime form of Lord Nṛsiṁha-deva."

47. Nāgas: "Sinful Hiraṇyakaśipu took away our jewels and our wives. Now, You are the source of all pleasure to our wives. We together offer You obeisances."

48. Manus: "Due to the demon, our laws for maintaining *varṇāśrama-dharma* were destroyed. Now that You have killed this great demon, we are in our normal condition. Kindly instruct us, Your eternal servants."

49. Prajāpatis: "This demon forbade us to create any more good progeny. Now he is lying dead. Let us offer obeisances unto You, whose incarnation is meant for the welfare of the entire universe."

50. Gandharvas: "Our singing and dancing is meant to please You. But this demon has made us to dance and sing for him. Now he got a low condition, the activities of such an upstart cannot have any benefit."

51. Cāraṇas: "As You have destroyed the demon, we are now relieved, and we eternally take shelter of Your lotus feet, which award liberation from material world."

52. Yakṣas: "Even though we are Your best servants, this demon engaged us as palanquin carriers. But now You have killed this demon who is a trouble to everyone."

53. Kimpuruṣas: "We are insignificant and cannot offer suitable prayers unto You, the Supreme Lord. When devotees got disgusted by this demon, You killed him."

54. Vaitālikas: "This demon usurped our position of chanting Your spotless glories in great assemblies. Now, You made us fortunate by killing this sinful demon who was like a chronic disease."

55. Kinnaras: "Even though we are Your ever-existing servants, this demon engaged us in his service without remuneration. Now You killed him. Please continue to be our patron."

56. Associates of Lord Viṣṇu: "Your wonderful form is meant for the good fortune of all worlds. This Hiraṇyakaśipu was the same Jaya (Your doorkeeper), who was cursed by *brāhmaṇas*. We understand that his killing is Your special mercy upon him."

7.9 Prahlāda Pacifies Lord Nṛsiṁha-deva with Prayers

7.9 Prahlāda pacifies Lord Nṛsiṁhadeva with prayers
- 1-7: The demigods request Prahlāda to appease the angry Lord
- 8-50: Prayers of Prahlāda Mahārāja (Summary chart inside)
- 51-55: Lord Nṛsiṁha's reply to Prahlāda's prayers

When the demigods failed to appease Lord Nṛsiṁha, Prahlāda pacifies Him with prayers.

1-7: The Demigods Request Prahlāda to Appease the Angry Lord

1. The demigods dared not to approach Lord Nṛsiṁha-deva at that time because He was absorbed in the mood of anger.

2. Even Lakṣmī couldn't approach the Lord even though requested by the demigods, saying that she had never seen such an astonishing (*mahad adbhutam*) form before.

Influence of līlā-śaktī: The Lord has unlimited eternal forms in Vaikuṇṭha and Lakṣmī had certainly seen Nṛsiṁha in some previous *kalpa*. Her impression of not having previously seen or heard about this form is inspired by *līlā-śakti* or the Lord's pastime potency, in order to make everyone taste *adbhuta-rasa*, the mood of astonishment.

Lord Nṛsiṁha's anger couldn't be pacfied by Brahmā, Śiva and even Lakṣmī, because the Lord wanted to exhibit His affection for Prahlāda and give him the opportunity to pacify Him.

3. Brahmā requested Prahlāda to go forward and appease the angry Lord Nṛsiṁha.

4. Little Prahlāda proceeded toward the Lord and fell at His feet to offer obeisances.

5. Lord Nṛsiṁha-deva's ecstatic affection for Prahlāda	
sva-pāda-mūle patitaṁ tam arbhakaṁ	When the small boy Prahlāda prostrated at the soles of His lotus feet
vilokya devaḥ kṛpayā pariplutaḥ	Lord Nṛsiṁha-deva saw him and became overwhelmed with affection for him

utthāpya tac-chīrṣṇy adadhāt karāmbujaṁ	Raising Prahlāda, the Lord placed His lotus hand upon the boy's head, because
kālāhi-vitrasta-dhiyāṁ kṛtābhayam	**His hand creates fearlessness** to those whose minds are afraid of the snake of time

6. Prahlāda's symptoms of ecstasy	
sa tat-kara-sparśa-dhutākhilāśubhaḥ	By the touch of Lord's hand, Prahlāda was completely freed of all material contamination.
sapady abhivyakta-parātma-darśanaḥ	He immediately manifested realization of the Supreme Soul.
tat-pāda-padmaṁ hṛdi nirvṛto dadhau	In transcendental bliss, He captured the Lord's lotus feet within the core of his heart.
hṛṣyat-tanuḥ klinna-hṛd-aśru-locanaḥ	His body showed ecstatic symptoms, his heart was softened with love, and his eyes with tears.

7. Prahlāda's mood in beginning prayers	
astauṣīd dharim ekāgra-manasā susamāhitaḥ	Prahlāda began his prayers to Hari with focussed mind and full attention
prema-gadgadayā vācā	with love and in a faltering voice
tan-nyasta-hṛdayekṣaṇaḥ	by fixing his heart and sight on Lord Nṛsiṁha.

Ability to fix one's mind (*samādhi*) upon lotus feet is a result of *yoga-siddhi*, attained when one is freed from all material diversions.

8-50: Prayers of Prahlāda Mahārāja

8-12: Prahlāda prepares himself to offer prayers

8. How can I satisfy You when devas and munis failed?	
brahmādayaḥ sura-gaṇā munayo 'tha siddhāḥ	Great demigods headed by Brahmā, great sages and perfected beings
sattvaikatāna-gatayo vacasāṁ pravāhaiḥ	who are immersed in mode of goodness, and who praised with streams of excellent words
nārādhituṁ puru-guṇair adhunāpi pipruḥ	could not satisfy the Lord up till now, although they all are well qualified.
kiṁ toṣṭum arhati sa me harir ugra-jāteḥ	How is it possible for me, who have been born in a family of demons, to offer suitable prayers to satisfy Him?

Vaiṣṇava humility: A Vaiṣṇava who is fully qualified to serve the Lord still thinks himself extremely low while offering prayers. One should not be falsely proud of his Vaiṣṇava qualifications. Unless one is meek and humble, progress in spiritual life is difficult.

Having said that *sattva* (mode of goodness) and *vacasāṁ pravāha* (eloquent praises) are not sufficient to please the Lord, Prahlāda will enumerate other external qualifications by which one cannot satisfy the Lord. Only *bhakti* can please Him.

9. No material qualification can satisfy You, only bhakti can	
manye dhanābhijana-rūpa-tapaḥ-śrutaujas-	I consider – (*i*) wealth (*ii*) an aristocratic family (*iii*) beauty (*iv*) austerity (*v*) education (*vi*) sensory expertise
tejaḥ-prabhāva-bala-pauruṣa-buddhi-yogāḥ	(*vii*) lustre (*viii*) influence (*ix*) physical strength (*x*) diligence (*xi*) intelligence and (*xii*) mystic yogic power
nārādhanāya hi bhavanti parasya puṁso	– not as qualifications by which one cannot satisfy the Supreme Personality of Godhead.
bhaktyā tutoṣa bhagavān gaja-yūtha-pāya	One can satisfy Him simply by devotional service. He was satisfied by Gajendra, king of elephants, who had devotion.

10. A low-born devotee is better than a brāhmaṇa nondevotee	
viprād dvi-ṣaḍ-guṇa-yutād aravinda-nābha-pādāravinda-vimukhāt śvapacaṁ variṣṭham	If a *brāhmaṇa* has all the twelve brahminical qualifications[6] (or the twelve qualities mentioned in the previous verse), but is averse to the lotus feet of the lotus-naveled Lord, he is certainly lower than a devotee who is a dog-eater.
manye tad-arpita-mano-vacanehitārtha-	I consider that devotee, who has dedicated his mind, words, activities, wealth and life to the Lord, to be better.
prāṇaṁ punāti sa kulaṁ na tu bhūrimānaḥ	Such a devotee can purify his whole family, whereas the so-called *brāhmaṇa* cannot purify even himself.

Hearing Prahlāda say that one who has dedicated everthing to the Lord is great, the Lord might question him, "Am I self-centered, because I am pleased with *bhakti* unto Me and not with others?" Anticipating such a question Prahlāda speaks –

[6] **The twelve brahminical qualities** mentioned in *Sanat-sujāta* are – knowledge, truth, mind control, sense control, hearing, detachment, shyness, tolerance, non-envy, sacrifice, charity, fortitude, and peacefulness.

jñānaṁ ca satyaṁ ca damaḥ śrutaṁ ca hy amātsaryaṁ hrīs titikṣānasūyā
yajñaś ca dānaṁ ca dhṛtiḥ śamaś ca mahā-vratā dvādaśa brāhmaṇasya

11. Our offerings are for our benefit, not Yours	
naivātmanaḥ prabhur ayaṁ nija-lābha-pūrṇo	The offerings made to the Lord are not meant for His own benefit as He is always fully satisfied in Himself.
mānaṁ janād aviduṣaḥ karuṇo vṛṇīte	The Lord mercifully accepts respect from an ignorant person.
yad yaj jano bhagavate vidadhīta mānaṁ	Whatever worship a person offers to the Supreme Personality of Godhead,
tac cātmane prati-mukhasya yathā mukha-śrīḥ	is for that person's benefit, just as the beauty of a face produces a beautiful reflection.

The Lord is always glorious, whether the devotee glorifies Him or not, but if the devotee engages in glorifying the Lord, the devotee automatically becomes glorious.

Prahlāda's confusions are gone. Since the Lord is pleased by *bhakti*, and not by good birth or wealth, and since respecting Him is beneficial for all, Prahlāda decided to praise the Lord's glories, without consideration of his material position such as low-birth.

12. I will offer prayers as per my ability, for my purification	
tasmād ahaṁ vigata-viklava īśvarasya	Therefore, having given up the contemplation of being unfit, I offer prayers to the Supreme controller,
sarvātmanā mahi gṛṇāmi yathā manīṣam	in full surrender and endeavor, as far as my intelligence allows.
nīco 'jayā guṇa-visargam anupraviṣṭaḥ	Anyone who has been forced by ignorance to enter the material world
pūyeta yena hi pumān anuvarṇitena	may be purified of material life if he offers prayers to the Lord and hears His glories.

Having made up his mind to offer prayers for his own purification, Prahlāda humbly begins his prayers. He once again describes his lower position compared to the demigods.

13-14: Requesting the Lord to give up His anger

13a. The demigods are not fearful like us. They are Your servants situated in *sattva*.

13b. Your pleasing incarnations (*rucira-avatāra*) are Your pastimes for Your pleasure (*ātma-sukhāya*) and for the protection and prosperity (*kṣemāya*) of the universe.

Such pastimes as those of Nṛsiṁha-deva are certainly not meant to create a fearful situation for the devotees, but nonetheless the devotees, being very simple and faithful, were afraid of the fierce incarnation. Therefore Prahlāda requests Lord to give up His anger.

14. Your present form causes fearlessness. Please give up anger.	
tad yaccha manyum asuraś ca hatas tvayādya	O Lord, please cease Your anger, now that Your have killed the demon (Hiraṇyakaśipu) today.
modeta sādhur api vṛścika-sarpa-hatyā	Even saintly persons take pleasure in the killing of a scorpion or a snake (because they are envious and unnecessarily give suffering to people).
lokāś ca nirvṛtim itāḥ pratiyanti sarve	All the worlds have achieved great satisfaction because of the death of this demon.
rūpaṁ nṛsiṁha vibhayāya janāḥ smaranti	They will always remember Your auspicious form of Nṛsiṁha in order to be free from fear.

Devotees are not afraid of the Lord's fearful form.

15-22: Seeking the Lord's shelter

15. I am not afraid of 'Your fearful form'	
nāhaṁ bibhemy ajita te 'tibhayānakāsya-	O unconquerable Lord, I am not afraid of Your most ferocious mouth,
jihvārka-netra-bhrukuṭī-rabhasogra-daṁṣṭrāt	tongue, bright sun-like eyes, frowning eyebrows, sharp and pinching teeth,
āntra-srajaḥ-kṣataja-keśara-śaṅku-karṇān	garland of intestines, bloody mane, or high, wedgelike ears.
nirhrāda-bhīta-digibhād ari-bhin-nakhāgrāt	Nor do I fear Your tumultuous roaring, which makes elephants flee, or Your nails that pierce the enemy.

Fearlessness by seeking shelter: Nṛsiṁha-deva's fierce appearance was certainly most dangerous for nondevotees, but not for surrendered devotees. Lion is fearsome for other animals, not for its cubs. Seawater is dreadful for all the living entities on land, but not for a fish. Because it has taken shelter of the big ocean. Great elephants are taken away by flooding waters of river, but a small fish can swim opposite the current.

Although Prahlāda wasn't afraid of the Lord's fearful form, he was afraid of the material existence (*samsāra*) that produces aversion towards the Lord. Actually Prahlāda, being a pure devotee, is not fearful of this world, but he was just representing a conditined soul.

16. I am afraid of conditioned life. I need Your shelter.	
trasto 'smy ahaṁ kṛpaṇa-vatsala duḥsahogra-	O Lord, who are kind to the fallen souls! I am afraind of the intolerable and ferocious
saṁsāra-cakra-kadanād grasatāṁ praṇītaḥ	cycle of birth and death. I am thrown in to the association of devouring demons and

baddhaḥ sva-karmabhir uśattama te 'ṅghri-mūlaṁ prīto 'pavarga-śaraṇaṁ hvayase kadā nu	bound by the reactions of my past deeds. O insurmountable Lord, when will You will call me to the shelter of Your lotus feet, the ultimate goal for liberation?

The Lord might say to Prahlāda, "What will you do by serving My feet? Please enjoy the happiness from the wealth of the three worlds conquered by your father."

17. Material dualities and miserable remedies	
yasmāt priyāpriya-viyoga-saṁyoga-janma-	Because of this material existence I am experiencing pleasing and displeasing circumstances, and separation and meeting with friends and enemies.
śokāgninā sakala-yoniṣu dahyamānaḥ	I am suffering in every form of life, as if burning in the fire of lamentation.
duḥkhauṣadhaṁ tad api duḥkham atad-dhiyāhaṁ	The remedies for material miseries are more miserable than the miseries themselves.
bhūman bhramāmi vada me tava dāsya-yogam	O great Lord, kindly instruct me, who is wandering in the cycle of birth and death, in Your divine service.

The only remedy for all the material miseries is to render service to the Supreme Lord. Whether one is in heavenly or hellish planets or is a rich or a poor man, no material condition is pleasing. In material life, both misery and happiness are ultimately miserable. If one wants uncontaminated pleasure, he must engage in the Lord's service.

The Lord might say to Prahlāda, "Though you attain service to Me, still you should seek out some other solution for the material miseries." - Prahlāda reveals some anger and pride now.

18. Devotee's life and duty: To glorify the Lord in paramparā	
so 'haṁ priyasya suhṛdaḥ paradevatāyā līlā-kathās tava nṛsiṁha viriñca-gītāḥ	O my Lord Nṛsiṁha, my dearmost well-wisher. I shall chant Your glories, following the footsteps of Lord Brahmā and his disciplic succession.
añjas titarmy anugṛṇan guṇa-vipramukto	By such glorification, I shall easily be purified of the contamination of material modes and cross
durgāṇi te pada-yugālaya-haṁsa-saṅgaḥ	over all the miserable conditions of material life. I shall serve You in the association of liberated devotees who constantly meditate on Your feet.

Advancing in spiritual life also involves *tapasya* or voluntary acceptance of some inconvenience – which is not as dangerous as material attempts to mitigate all miseries.

19. Lord Nṛsiṁha is the only shelter	
bālasya neha śaraṇaṁ pitarau nṛsiṁha	My Lord Nṛsiṁha-deva! (*i*) A father and mother cannot protect their child.
nārtasya cāgadam udanvati majjato nauḥ	(*ii*) A doctor and medicine cannot relieve a patient. (*iii*) A boat on the ocean cannot protect a drowning man.
taptasya tat-pratividhir ya ihāñjaseṣṭas	The remedies accepted by people for their miseries in this world are not a shelter at all.
tāvad vibho tanu-bhṛtāṁ tvad-upekṣitānām	O Lord, embodied souls who do not accept You or not cared for by You can't do anything for their betterment.

One should depend fully on the causeless mercy of the Lord. Although as a matter of routine duty one must, of course, accept other remedial measures, no one can protect one who is neglected by the Supreme Lord.

Why the conditioned souls cannot do anything for their betterment?

20. Your energies manifest everything including the cause for which people work, the place where they work, the time when they work, the matter due to which they work, the goal of their life, and the process of obtaining that goal. Indeed, since the energy and energetic are identical, all of them are but manifestations of You.

The Lord might ask, "If I am the form of everything, then I am also *saṁsāra*. Why then do you want liberation from My form of *saṁsāra*?" Prahlāda answers this in next two verses.

21. Your shelter liberates us from māyā: By Your *puruṣa* expansion, You have created the subtle bodies of the *jīvas* through *māyā*, agitated by time (*kāla*). Thus the mind entraps the *jīva* in unlimited desires to be fulfilled by Vedic directions and sixteen elements. Who can get free from this wheel of *saṁsāra* unless he takes Your shelter?

Why only the Lord can save the entangled conditioned souls?

22. You are the controller of māyā and are never conquered by the material qualities. The time element is Your representation. I am being crushed by the wheel of time (*niṣpīḍyamānam*). Kindly take me under Your protection (*upakarṣa vibho*). I surrender unto You (*prapannam*).

Prahlāda was not giving importance to this material world because he had the previous experience of seeing his father's suffering.

23-25: Experience of seeing the futility of material pleasures

23. I have seen the futility of āyu, śriya and vibhava i.e., long life, opulence and power of the demigods, which people desire. Simply by the movements of my fathers' eyebrows in anger, the demigods were vanquished. Yet my powerful father has now been vanquished by You within a moment.

The Lord might ask Prahlāda, "So what do you want?"

24. Let me serve Your pure devotee	
tasmād amūs tanu-bhṛtām aham āśiṣo 'jña āyuḥ śriyaṁ vibhavam aindriyam āviriñcyāt	Therefore, I have full experience of the futility of worldly opulence, mystic power, longevity and other material pleasures enjoyed by all living entities, from Lord Brahmā down to the ant.
necchāmi te vilulitān uruvikrameṇa kālātmanopanaya māṁ nija-bhṛtya-pārśvam	So, I do not desire them. As time, You destroy them all. Please take me to the side of Your pure devotee and let me serve him as a sincere servant.

The Lord might ask Prahlāda, "What is this? Everyone desires enjoyment and power and you are rejecting them?"

25. The happiness of this material world is insubstantial	
kutrāśiṣaḥ śruti-sukhā mṛgatṛṣṇi-rūpāḥ	What is the use of material benedictions, which are pleasant only to hear about, like a mirage in the desert?
kvedaṁ kalevaram aśeṣa-rujāṁ virohaḥ	What is the value of material body, which is merely a source of unlimited diseases?
nirvidyate na tu jano yad apīti vidvān	The so-called philosophers, scientists and politicians know this very well, yet they aspire for temporary happiness.
kāmānalaṁ madhu-lavaiḥ śamayan durāpaiḥ	They pacify the fire of desire by a drop of hard-earned happiness, but do not become detached.

Prahlāda acknowledges the special mercy that Lord Nṛsiṁha had showed upon him.

26-29: The Supreme Lord's mercy

26. You have mercifully put You hand on my head	
kvāhaṁ rajaḥ-prabhava īśa tamo 'dhike 'smin jātaḥ suretara-kule kva tavānukampā	O Lord, where am I, who was born in a family of demons full of passion and ignorance? What is to be said of Your causeless mercy
na brahmaṇo na tu bhavasya na vai ramāyā	which was never offered even to Brahmā, Śiva or Lakṣmī? (You never put Your hand on their heads)
yan me 'rpitaḥ śirasi padma-karaḥ prasādaḥ	You placed Your merciful lotus hand upon my head (and made me the greatest though I am low).

Bhakti is so great that when it is offered even by those born in low families, the Supreme Lord accepts it as being more valuable than the service offered even by the goddess of fortune, His constant companion.

The Lord's causeless mercy may be bestowed upon anyone, regardless of one's material position. Everyone is eligible to worship the Lord, irrespective of one's material position.

27. You are reciprocal, not partial	
naiṣā parāvara-matir bhavato nanu syāj	You do not discriminate by high or low birth
jantor yathātma-suhṛdo jagatas tathāpi	like the ordinary people, because You are the friend of the whole universe. Still,
saṁsevayā surataror iva te prasādaḥ	You reciprocate according to the level of one's service, exactly as a desire tree.
sevānurūpam udayo na parāvaratvam	Your mercy is according to the degree of service, and not by high or low birth.

The Lord is impartial in fulfilling everyone's desires. The living entity is the creator of one's own destiny. One's relationship with the Lord is in proportion to one's surrender and service. The higher or lower positions of the living entities are selected by the living entities themselves by their own desires and actions. The Lord is not responsible for their higher or lower grades of existence (BG 9.25: *yānti deva-vratā devān...*).

The Lord might ask Prahlāda, "You have said that service to Me is the cause of My mercy to you. You have excluded favoritism by the example of desire tree. But what is the cause of this service by a devotee?"

28. I want to serve Nārada Muni who saved me	
evaṁ janaṁ nipatitaṁ prabhavāhi-kūpe	I was gradually falling into a blind well full of snakes, following the general populace.
kāmābhikāmam anu yaḥ prapatan prasaṅgāt	Because of my association with material desires, one after another, I was falling down.
kṛtvātmasāt surarṣiṇā bhagavan gṛhītaḥ	But Your servant Nārada Muni accepted me as his disciple and made me achieve spiritual position. O Lord!
so 'haṁ kathaṁ nu visṛje tava bhṛtya-sevām	How can I give up service to your servant? It is my first duty to serve him.

One should first serve the guru, so that by his mercy one is qualified to serve the Supreme Lord. One should not bypass the spiritual master and desire to serve the Lord directly, by concoction. This is not the principle for a Vaiṣṇava.

29. You proved Your devotee Nārada's words true by saving me and killing my father, O unlimited Lord! Taking his sword, my father told me, "Let your Lord protect you! I will cut off your head."

30-38: The Supreme Lord and the cosmos

30. Whatever exits is You alone, as through Your *māyā* and the three modes, You create, maintain and destroy this universe and yet You exist beyond it.

Energy in which the Lord's all-pervasiveness is not realized is called material. Otherwise, everything is spiritual.

31. You and the cosmos are related as the seed and the tree, or the subtle cause and the gross manifestation. You are the universe, its cause and its effect, yet you are different from it. You also cause its annihilation. The conception of 'mine and yours' is illusory (*māyā*).

In the next five verses, Prahlāda elaborates on the Lord being the cause of the universe, being situated at its beginning, middle and end.

32. As Kāraṇodakaśāyī Viṣṇu, You place the universe within You after its annihilation, and appear to sleep (*yoga-nidra*) in the casual ocean, enjoying spiritual bliss (in *turiya* stage), without interest in material objects.

33. As Garbhodakaśāyī Viṣṇu, You awaken from the bed of Ananta, and from Your navel the seed of the lotus of universe is manifested, like a banyan tree grows from a seed. This universe, Your body, composed of the modes of *prakṛti*, which was merged in Your body, was agitated by Your time energy (*kāla-śakti*) to come out like this.

34. Brahmā appeared from that lotus and he dove into the water to find the source of the lotus for one hundred years. He could find no trace of You, however, for when a seed fructifies, the original seed cannot be seen.

35. Brahmā did severe austerities and after thus being purified, he could see You, the cause of all causes, within himself, spread throughout his own body and senses, just as aroma is perceived in the earth.

36. Brahmā saw Your form with thousands of faces, feet, heads, hands, thighs, noses, ears and eyes (*mahā-puruṣa*). Thus he achieved transcendental bliss.

37. You appeared as Hayagrīva, with the head of a horse (*haya-śira*), You killed the demons Madhu and Kaiṭabha (in *raja* and *tama*) and gave the Vedas to Brahmā. The sages honor Your forms as transcendental, untinged by material qualities (*sattva*).

38. Your various incarnations; You are triyuga	
itthaṁ nṛ-tiryag-ṛṣi-deva-jhaṣāvatārair	In this way, You incarnate as a human being (Rāma), an animal (Varāha), a saint (Paraśurāma), a demigod (Vāmana), an aquatic (Matsya and Kūrma),

lokān vibhāvayasi haṁsi jagat pratīpān	thus maintaining the entire creation in different planetary systems and killing the demoniac principles.
dharmaṁ mahā-puruṣa pāsi yugānuvṛttaṁ	According to the age, O my Lord, You protect the principles of religion.
channaḥ kalau yad abhavas tri-yugo 'tha sa tvam	In Kali yuga, You do not assert Yourself as the Supreme Lord (Śrī Caitanya Mahāprabhu), and thus You are known as Triyuga, or the Lord who appears in three *yugas*.

Representing a common man, Prahlāda humbly asks the Lord, "Constantly appearing, You shower the nectar of Your form, qualities and pastimes. But my sinful mind does not take pleasure in this. What shall I do?" In this mood Prahlāda speaks the next three verses.

39-45: Prahlāda's humility and concern for fallen souls

39. Sinful state of the material mind	
naitan manas tava kathāsu vikuṇṭha-nātha saṁprīyate durita-duṣṭam asādhu tīvram	O Lord of Vaikuṇṭha, my uncontrollable and dishonest mind is polluted by sinful activities, and is not satisfied with Your topics.
kāmāturaṁ harṣa-śoka-bhayaiṣaṇārtaṁ	It is afflicted by lust, so-called joy, distress, lamentation, fear and desire for money.
tasmin kathaṁ tava gatiṁ vimṛśāmi dīnaḥ	In such a mental status, how then can this wretch think of Your activities?

In the next verse, Prahlāda gives the reason why his mind has become so sinful.

40. Embarrassment by ever-distracted senses	
jihvaikato 'cyuta vikarṣati māvitṛptā	O infallible Lord, my unsatisfied **tongue** pulls me to palatable dishes,
śiśno 'nyatas *tvag-* *udaraṁ* *śravaṇaṁ kutaścit*	my **genitals** pull me for sex, my **skin** pulls me to touch soft things, my **belly** wants to eat more, my **ear** is attracted to mundane music,
ghrāṇo 'nyataś capala-dṛk kva ca karma-śaktir	my sense of **smell** pulls in another way, my restless **eyes** want to see scenes of sense gratification, and my **active senses** are attracted elsewhere.
bahvyaḥ sapatnya iva geha-patiṁ lunanti	I am like a person with many wives, each pulling him in her own way. (Thus I have no time for chanting Your glories.)

Prahlāda, a pure Vaiṣṇava, prays not only for himself but for the deliverance of all other living entities suffering in this material world.

41. O Lord, You are on the other side of Vaitaraṇī, the river of death. Due to our *karma*, we have fallen into this river and are fearful, suffering the pains of birth and death. Now by Your causeless mercy and compassion, help us cross this river.

Here, Prahlāda is not praying for his own deleverance only, but for everyone's. There are two classes of Vaiṣṇavas – (*i*) *Bhajanānandīs,* who worship the Lord for their own benefit and (*ii*) *Goṣṭhy-ānandīs,* who try to elevate all others to Kṛṣṇa consciousness.

42. Compassionately deliver us all: O original *guru* of the world (*akhila-guro*), what is difficult for You, who manage the universal affairs, in delivering fallen souls? You are the friend of suffering humanity (*ārta-bandho*). Great people are merciful to the foolish.

Prahlāda says, "But why do You have to deliver us, my Lord? We simply serve Your dear devotees and get delivered."

43. I am fearless, but concerned about the fools	
naivodvije para duratyaya-vaitaraṇyās	I am not at all disturbed or afraid of the insurmountable material existence or Vaitaraṇi river.
tvad-vīrya-gāyana-mahāmṛta-magna-cittaḥ	Because my consciousness is fully absorbed in the nectarean bliss of chanting Your glories.
śoce tato vimukha-cetasa indriyārtha-	I simply lament for those who are averse to You and making plans for sense gratification.
māyā-sukhāya bharam udvahato vimūḍhān	Such fools carry the burden of illusory happiness in maintaining their families, societies and countries.

Prahlāda's happiness and distress: Prahlāda felt transcendental bliss because of his being Kṛṣṇa conscious, yet he felt great unhappiness for fools who make elaborate plans to be happy in this material world.

44. I don't wish to be delivered alone, leaving these fools	
prāyeṇa deva munayaḥ sva-vimukti-kāmā	O Lord! I see many sages are generally interested only in their own deliverance.
maunaṁ caranti vijane na parārtha-niṣṭhāḥ	They practice silence, and wander in solitary places (Himalayas), not caring for the deliverance of others.
naitān vihāya kṛpaṇān vimumukṣa eko	As for me, however, I do not wish to be liberated alone, leaving aside all these poor fools.
nānyaṁ tvad asya śaraṇaṁ bhramato 'nupaśye	I do not see any shelter other than You for those wandering blindly in this world.

45. The insignificant happiness of gṛhamedhis	
yan maithunādi-gṛhamedhi-sukhaṁ hi tucchaṁ	The material happiness of household life and sex life is insignificant.
kaṇḍūyanena karayor iva duḥkha-duḥkham	It is like the increased suffering created by rubbing itchy hands together.
tṛpyanti neha kṛpaṇā bahu-duḥkha-bhājaḥ	Despite such suffering, the lusty fools are not satisfied by repeated sense enjoyment.
kaṇḍūtivan manasijaṁ viṣaheta dhīraḥ	Knowing that the pleasure of such itch is only a mental concoction, the sober people tolerate it.

46-50: Bhakti, the ultimate refuge

46. The ten methods namely, silence (*mauna*), vows (*vrata*), Vedic knowledge (*śruta*), austerity (*tapa*), scriptural study (*adhyayana*), occupational duty (*sva-dharma*), to explain *śāstras* (*vyākhya*), living alone (*raha*), *japa,* and trance (*samādhi*), are generally a professional practice and means of livelihood for those who cannot control senses.

47. Your energy manifests the cosmos and all forms of cause and effect within it. Just as a wise man can see how fire pervades wood, those engaged in *bhakti* understand how You are both the cause and effect.

48. You are everything subtle and gross – including the air, earth, fire, sky, water, sense objects, life airs, five senses, mind, consciousness and false ego. Anything expressed, either by the words or by the mind, are nothing but You.

49. No one can understand You, including the three modes and their controlling deities, the five gross elements, mind, demigods, human beings, because they are all subject to birth and annihilation (*martya*). Considering this, the wise (*sudhiya*) engage in *bhakti*.

Since one cannot know the Lord by study and other methods, giving up efforts to know Him, one should strive to perform *sādhana* for *prema* unto Him. Prahlāda Mahārāja summarizes his prayers in the last verse.

50. The six kinds of bhakti are offering prayers (*stuti*), dedicating results of activities (*karma*), worshiping (*pūja*), working on Your behalf (*karma*), remembering Your lotus feet (*smṛtiś caraṇayoḥ*) and hearing Your glories (*śravaṇaṁ kathāyām*). How can one attain *prema* without these six types of *bhakti?*

8-50: Prahlāda Mahārāja's Prayers At A Glance

8-12: Preparing to pray

- 8. How can I satisfy You, when devas and munis failed?
- 9. No material qualification can satisfy You, only bhakti can
- 10. A low-born devotee is better than a brāhmaṇa non-devotee
- 11. Our offerings are for our benefit, not for Your benefit
- 12. I will offer prayers as per my ability, for my purification

13-14: Request to give up anger

- 13a. Demigods are not fearful like us.
- 13b. You incarnate for Your pleasure pastimes and protection of the universe
- 14. Your present form causes fearlessness. Please give up anger.

15-22: Seeking the Lord's shelter

- 15. I am not afraid of 'Your fearful form'
- 16. I am afraid of conditioned life. I need Your shelter.
- 17. Material dualities have miserable remedies. Only remedy is Your service.
- 18. I will chant Your glories in paramparā and cross this nescience
- 19. Lord Nṛsiṁha is the only shelter
- 20. Your energies manifest everything
- 21. Your shelter liberates us from māyā
- 22. You are the controller of māyā, so only You can deliver us

23-25: Previous experience

- 23. I have seen the futility of *āyu*, *śriya* and *vibhava* of my father
- 24. Let me serve Your pure devotee sincerely
- 25. The happiness of this world is insubstantial

26-29: The Supreme Lord's mercy

- 26. You have mercifully put You hand on my head (not on Lakṣmī, Śiva, Brahmā)
- 27. You are reciprocal, not partial
- 28. I want to serve Nārada Muni who saved me
- 29. You proved Your devotee Nārada's words true by saving me

30-38: The Lord and the cosmos

- 30. Whatever exits is You alone
- 31. You and the cosmos are related, but You are aloof
- 32. As Mahā-viṣṇu, Your *yoga-nidra* is transcendental
- 33-36. As Garbhodakaśāyī Viṣṇu, You gave birth to Brahmā who did *tapasya* and saw You
- 37. As Hayagriva You gave the Vedas to Brahmā
- 38. You are triyuga

39-45: Prahlāda's humility and concern for fallen souls

- 39. Sinful state of the material mind
- 40. Embarrassment by ever-distracted senses
- 41. Please help us cross this Vaitaraṇī river
- 42. Compassionately deliver us all
- 43. I am fearless, but concerned about the fools
- 44. I don't wish to be delivered alone, leaving these fools
- 45. The insignificant happiness of gṛhamedhis

46-50: Bhakti, the ultimate refuge

- 46. The ten methods on the path of liberation are just professional practice
- 47. Only by bhakti, we understand that Your energy manifests all causes and effects
- 48. You are everything, subtle and gross
- 49. Martyas can't understand You; So, sudhiyas engage in bhakti
- 50. The six kinds of bhakti

51-55: Lord Nṛsiṁha's Reply to Prahlāda's Prayers

51. Nṛsiṁha-deva pacified: When Prahlāda described the qualities (*guṇa*) of Nṛsiṁha-deva, who is devoid of material qualities (*nirguṇa*), the Lord gave up anger and spoke as follows:

52. I am pleased, ask for a boon: "Gentle Prahlāda, all good fortune unto you. I am pleased with you. I fulfill the desires of all, you may ask from Me any benediction.

53. Seeing Me is very rare for those who do not please Me. But one who has seen or pleased Me has nothing more to lament for one's satisfaction. May you live long.

mām aprīṇata āyuṣman darśanaṁ durlabhaṁ hi me
dṛṣṭvā māṁ na punar jantur ātmānaṁ taptum arhati

54. Only I can fulfill everyone's desires. Therefore the wise try to please Me in all different *rasas* (mellows), for I am the master of all blessings.

prīṇanti hy atha māṁ dhīrāḥ sarva-bhāvena sādhavaḥ
śreyas-kāmā mahā-bhāga sarvāsām āśiṣām patim

55. Prahlāda didn't desire any material boon, though he was born in demoniac family and was allured by the Lord. It was due to his unalloyed *bhakti*.

7.10 Prahlāda, The Best Among Exalted Devotees

- **1-10:** Prahlāda Mahārāja refuses to accept material benedictions
  - 1-6: Prahlāda told Nṛsiṁhadeva, "Do not to tempt me with material boons. I am an unmotivated servant and not a merchant."
  - 7-10: Prahlāda desired not to have any material desires.
- **11-34:** Lord Nṛsiṁhadeva's instructions and Prahlāda coronation
  - 11-14: Lord Nṛsiṁhadeva instructs Prahlāda to enjoy opulences and perform bhakti-yoga
  - 15-17: Prahlāda prays for Hiraṇyakaśipu's deliverance
  - 18-23: Lord Nṛsiṁha glorifies the potency of devotees in purifying their dynasties
  - 24-29: Prahlāda performs the last rites of his father and Brahmā offers his prayers to Lord Nṛsiṁha
  - 30-34: Lord Nṛsiṁha cautions Brahmā not to give such benedictions to demons, and then departs.
- **35-50:** Nārada Muni concludes the narration
  - 35-40: The three births of Jaya and Vijaya
  - 41-50: Conclusion, Phala-śruti and glorification of Pandavas
- **51-70:** Lord Śiva destroys the three invisible cities of the demons
  - Maya Dānava constructed Tripura for the demons, who then defeated the demigods. With the help of Lord Kṛṣṇa, Lord Śiva dismantled Tripura, and became famous as Tripurāri.

1-10: Prahlāda Mahārāja Refuses To Accept Material Benedictions

1. Prahlāda considered the benedictions offered by Lord Nṛsiṁha-deva (in 7.9.52) to be impediments in *bhakti-yoga*. Thus he smiled and spoke as follows.

Prahlāda smiled and thought, "Tempting an ignorant boy, the Lord is testing me."

2. Don't tempt me with material boons	
mā māṁ pralobhayotpattyā	Please do not allure me; due to my demoniac birth,
saktaṁkāmeṣu tair varaiḥ	I am already attached to material enjoyment and boons.
tat-saṅga-bhīto nirviṇṇo	I am afraid of material association and I am detached from material desires.
mumukṣus tvām upāśritaḥ	I desire liberation and have taken Your shelter.

The ultimate goal of *bhakti* is not material achievements but love of Godhead. When one is allured by material possessions, they are considered to be given by *māyā*, but when one uses them for the Lord's service, they are considered God's gifts for enhancing *bhakti*.

Lord Nṛsiṁha might say, "Do I actually tempt My devotees?" Prahlāda responds, "Your intention is to show to everyone the highest standard of Your pure devotee."

3. Desiring to exhibit the symptoms of Your devotee, You have sent me to this world of lusty desires, the seed of material existence which creates knot in the heart.

The Supreme Lord has no desire to send His pure devotee to this material world, nor does a devotee have any material purpose in coming here. A pure devotee sets the best example for the common people to follow, by his behavior.

4. I am not a merchant: You are so kind that You could not induce a devotee to do something unbeneficial for him. One who desires material benefit in exchange for devotional service is no better than a merchant (*vaṇik*).

5. Pure servant and master: A servant who desires material profits is not a qualified servant. A master who bestows boons to maintain his position is not a pure master.

āśāsāno na vai bhṛtyaḥ svāminy āśiṣa ātmanaḥ
na svāmī bhṛtyataḥ svāmyam icchan yo rāti cāśiṣaḥ

The demigods, to keep their prestigious positions, offer their worshipers whatever boons they want. So, a demigod cannot become master, for the real master is the Supreme Lord.

6. I am Your unmotivated servant, (*ahaṁ tv akāmas tvad-bhaktas*) and You are my eternal master (*tvaṁ ca svāmy anapāśrayaḥ*) not 'dependant' on my service. We have no other relationship, like the material kings and their servants.

Lord Nṛsiṁha might say, "Please accept something to please Me."

7. May I not have any material desires	
yadi dāsyasi me kāmān	If You at all want to bestow a benediction that I
varāṁs tvaṁ varadarṣabha	desire, O best of the givers of benediction,
kāmānāṁ hṛdy asaṁrohaṁ	then I pray that within the core of my heart
bhavatas tu vṛṇe varam	let there be no material desires (I desire Your service only).

8. The negative effects of material desires	
indriyāṇi manaḥ prāṇa	The functions of one's senses, mind, life,
ātmā dharmo dhṛtir matiḥ	body, religion, patience, intelligence,
hrīḥ śrīs tejaḥ smṛtiḥ satyaṁ	shyness, wealth, strength, memory and truthfulness
yasya naśyanti janmanā	are all destroyed from the very beginning of one's birth.

Material life means to be afflicted by a formidable disease called lusty desire. Liberation means freedom from such lusty desires that cause repeated birth and death. Desirelessness means freedom from material desires. Unalloyed devotion to the service of the Lord is the only spiritual desire. To fulfill this desire, one must be free from material desires.

Lord Nṛsiṁha might say, "If you do not desire benedictions, then why do you desire service to Me, saying that you want to be My servant?"

9. When one is able to give up all material desires, he becomes eligible to possess opulence like Yours (*bhagavattva*).

Bhagavattva does not mean becoming one with the Lord or exactly equal to Him. The servant in the spiritual world is engaged in Lord's service as a servant, friend, father, mother or conjugal lover, all of whom are equally as opulent as the Lord. This is *acintya-bhedābheda-tattva*. The master and servant are different yet equal in opulence.

Achieving the platform of *bhagavattva*, or being as good as the Supreme Person, does not mean that the devotee loses his position as a servant. A pure devotee, although as opulent as the Lord, is still meant to offer respectful obeisances to the Lord in service.

10. I offer respects to the Lord, full of six qualities, the Supreme Person, the Supreme soul, killer of all miseries, the wonderful lion and man, Brahman and Paramātmā.

oṁ namo bhagavate tubhyaṁ puruṣāya mahātmane
haraye 'dbhuta-siṁhāya brahmaṇe paramātmane

11-34: Lord Nṛsiṁha-deva's Instructions and Prahlāda Coronation

11-14: Lord Nṛsiṁha-deva's instructions to Prahlāda

11. Enjoy opulences: A devotee like you never desires material benedictions. Yet I order you to enjoy as the king of demons until the end of this *manvantara* (seventy-one *yuga* cycles, each of which equals 4,300,000 years).

Prahlāda Mahārāja might ask, "Because of what offense are You throwing me in the hole of material life?"

12. Perform bhakti-yoga: It does not matter that you are in the material world. You should always hear My topics and be absorbed in My thought. Give up fruitive activities (*karma-yoga*) and worship Me (*bhakti-yoga*).

Lord Nṛsiṁha tells Prahlāda, "Don't worry about *karma*. You are a *jīvan-mukta*, already liberated in this very life even in the material body."

13. Process of liberation from bondage	
bhogena puṇyaṁ kuśalena pāpaṁ	Having given up piety by enjoyment, sin by pious acts
kalevaraṁ kāla-javena hitvā	and material body by passage of time –
kīrtiṁ viśuddhāṁ sura-loka-gītāṁ	Your pure glory will be sung in heavenly planets.
vitāya māṁ eṣyasi mukta-bandhaḥ	You will be free from bondage and will come to Me.

Prahlāda, like Nārada Muni, was partly *sādhana-siddha* (one who attains by performance of *bhakti*) and partly *nitya-siddha* (one who is eternally perfect). This means they are *nitya-siddha* but also take forms of *sādhakas* during the pastimes.

Lord Nṛsiṁha said, "Not only you are free of bondage, but others who remember you become free of bondage as well."

14. One who remembers your activities and My activities, and who chants the prayers you have offered to Me, becomes free from the material reactions.

Previously Prahlāda prayed for the deliverance of all people suffering in this world. Now, he prays for the deliverance of one great sinner, his father. Although Hiraṇyakaśipu was purified as soon as he came in contact with Lord Nṛsiṁha's glance and lap, Prahlāda still wanted to hear from the Lord's own mouth that his father had been purified by His mercy.

15-17: Prahlāda prays for Hiraṇyakaśipu's deliverance

15-17. Prahlāda asks for a benediction, "Because You are merciful to the fallen, I ask You for only one benediction. Out of ignorance, My father thought that You killed his brother. He was angry at You, blasphemed You, and committed sins against me, Your devotee. I wish that he be excused for these sinful activities."

18-23: Lord Nṛsiṁha glorifies the potency of devotees

18. Dynasty purified: Your father has been purified, along with twenty-one forefathers. Because of your birth, your entire dynasty has been purified (*kula-pāvanaḥ*).

Prahlāda has purified both father's lineage and mother's lineage. When a Vaiṣṇava takes birth in a family, by the Lord's grace he purifies not only that family but also the families of his previous births.

19. Purification by devotees' presence	
yatra yatra ca mad-bhaktāḥ	Wherever and whenever there are My devotees
praśāntāḥ sama-darśinaḥ	who are peaceful, equipoised
sādhavaḥ samudācārās	well-behaved and endowed with all good qualities,
te pūyante 'pi kīkaṭāḥ	they purify even condemned dynasties and places.

20. Impartial and nonenvious: Because of love for Me, My devotees are free from material desires (*vigata-spṛha*), do not distinguish between lower and higher living entities, and are never jealous of anyone.

Prahlāda might say, "The greatness of those devotees is not astonishing to me. But I am not like that." The Lord says that Prahlāda is an exemplary devotee.

21. You are the best: Those who follow your example will naturally become My pure devotees. You are the best example of all devotees.

22. Father's funeral: Your father has already been purified by My touch at the time of his death. Perform his funeral rites. Having the best son, he will attain the best planets.

Although Hiraṇyakaśipu was already purified, he had to take birth on a higher planetary system to become a devotee again.

23. Take charge of your father's kingdom as directed by the *brāhmaṇas*. Fixing your mind upon Me (*mat-paraḥ*), perform your duties as a matter of formality.

A devotee is not obliged to follow Vedic regulative principles (See SB 11.5.41), but still he does them as a matter of ettiquette, to set example for common people. However, his faith is in the Supreme Lord and not in those rituals.

24. Prahlāda performed the death rituals for his father. Later he was then enthroned as the king by the *brāhmaṇas*.

25. Lord Brahmā, surrounded by the demigods, offered his prayers to Lord Nṛsiṁha.

26-29: Brahmā's prayers to Lord Nṛsiṁha

26. O Lord of all demigods (*deva-deva*), proprietor of the universe (*akhila-adhyakṣa*), cause of all living entities (*bhūta-bhāvana*) and original Lord (*pūrva-ja*)! By our good fortune, You have killed this sinful demon who was troubling the universe.

27. This demon received benediction from me that he wouldn't be killed by anyone within my creation. Proud of his austerity, he destroyed the Vedic system.

28. Prahlāda has been saved now from death. He is an exalted devotee and is now fully under Your protection.

29. If one meditates upon You, You naturally protect him from all sources of fear, including death.

30. Lord Nṛsiṁha to Brahmā, "It is dangerous to give benedictions to demons, just as it is dangerous to feed milk to a snake. I warn you not to give such benedictions to any demon again."

31. Being worshiped by Brahmā, the Lord then disappeared.

32. Prahlāda Mahārāja then worshiped all the demigods like Brahmā, Śiva and others.

33. Thereafter Brahmā made Prahlāda the king of all the demons.

34. The demigods offered benedictions to Prahlāda and returned to their abodes.

The discourse concerning Lord Nṛsiṁha and Prahlāda began when King Yudhiṣṭhira asked Nārada Muni how Śiśupāla and Dantavakra attained *sāyujya-mukti* (in 7.1.16-21). Thus Nārada told the story of their previous births. Now the story is concluded. Nārada will now relate how in three different births the associates of Lord Viṣṇu were killed by Viṣṇu Himself.

35-50: Nārada Muni Concludes the Narration

35-40: The three births of Jaya and Vijaya

35. First birth: Thus the two associates of Viṣṇu (Jaya and Vijaya) who became the sons of Diti (Hiraṇyakaśipu and Hiraṇyākṣa), were both killed. By illusion they had thought that the Supreme Lord was their enemy.

36-37. Second birth: They again took birth as Kumbhakarṇa and Rāvaṇa, and were killed by Lord Rāma. Both of them left their bodies, absorbed in thought of the Lord.

38. Third birth: They took birth again as Śiśupāla and Dantavakra and continued their enmity. It is they who merged into the body of the Lord.

39. Salvation by absorption: Many kings who acted as enemies of Kṛṣṇa attained salvation and received spiritual bodies, because they thought of the Lord at the time of death. This is similar to a worm becoming a wasp by meditating on the wasp.

40. Sārūpya mukti: Pure devotees receive *sārūpya-mukti* by practicing *bhakti*. Kings who thought of Kṛṣṇa as an enemy also achieved the same result.

41-50: Conclusion, Phala-śruti and glorification of Pandavas

41-42. Nārada concludes: I have explained what you (Yudhiṣṭhira) have asked about Śiśupāla's salvation. In this narration, various incarnations of the Lord, and the killing of the two demons have been described.

43-45. This narration describes –

- Mahā-bhāgavata Prahlāda's *bhakti*, *jñāna* and *varakti*
- The qualities and activities of the Supreme Lord
- *Bhāgavata-dharma*, the principles of religion by which one understands the Lord

46-47. Phala-śruti: One who faithfully hears and chants the narration of the activities and omnipotence of Lord Nṛsiṁha, the pure devotion of Prahlāda and the killing of Hiraṇyakaśpu is – liberated from material bondage and transferred to spiritual world.

A pure devotee always thinks himself to be the lowest, incompetent and unqualified. Thus after hearing the narration of Prahlāda, Yudhiṣṭhira, who was also on the same standard of *bhakti* as Prahlāda, lamented out of his humility, "Oh! Prahlāda was so fortunate to see the Lord. But we are not so fortunate!" Nārada immediately encouraged him as follows.

48. You (Pāṇḍavas) are most fortunate, for Kṛṣṇa personally lives in your palace, because He is attracted to you. Knowing this, great saints visit your house.

Although Lord Nṛsiṁha-deva appeared for Prahlāda, the Supreme Personality of Godhead in His original form as Kṛṣṇa was always living with the Pāṇḍavas. Nārada Muni said, "You Pāṇḍavas are more fortunate than Prahlāda, than me, his *guru*, than other devotees, than previous members of your dynasty like Yadu and Puru, than the sages like Vaśiṣṭha, Marīci and Kaśyapa, than Brahmā and Śiva. You are most fortunate among all *jīvas*. Kṛṣṇa does not personally live in human form in the houses of Prahlāda and others. And the sages do not come there to see Him!"

49. Kṛṣṇa is your intimate friend, cousin, constant well-wisher and spiritual master. He is the source of Brahman yet acts as your servant.

Yudhiṣṭhira might ask, "Why does the basis of Brahman act as a servant for the vision of material people like us?" Nārada Muni now explains the difficulty in understanding or describing about Kṛṣṇa's great powers and His being controlled by the devotees' *prema*.

50. Even Śiva and Brahmā could not properly describe the truth of the Supreme Lord. May the Lord be pleased with us.

Yudhiṣṭhira might ask, "Brahmā may not understand Kṛṣṇa, but Śiva can understand!" To explain this, Nārada narrates another story (that even Śiva derives power from Kṛṣṇa).

51-70: Lord Śiva Destroys the Three Invisible Cities of the Demons

51. Nārada Muni said, "Long long ago, Maya Dānava reduced the reputation of Lord Śiva. In that situation, the Supreme Lord Kṛṣṇa saved Lord Śiva."

52. Yudhiṣṭhira asked, "For what reason did Maya Dānava vanquish Lord Śiva's reputation? How did Lord Kṛṣṇa save Lord Śiva?"

Now Nārada Muni narrates the story of Śiva killing the demons with the help of Viṣṇu.

53. When the demigods defeated the demons, the demons took shelter of Maya Dānava.

54-56. Mystic Maya Dānava made three invisible residences resembling airplanes made of gold, silver and iron and gave them to the demons. Thus the demons remained invisible to the demigods and began to vanquish the three worlds. Then the rulers of those planets surrendered to Lord Śiva, for protection.

57-59a. Lord Śiva reassured the demigods and released his golden arrows that covered the three residential airplanes of the demons and the demons lost their lives.

59b-61. Maya Dānava revived the demons by putting their dead bodies into a well of nectar (*mṛta-sañjīvayitā*). The demons then became strong like thunderbolts and got up like lightening. Śiva became disappointed. Lord Viṣṇu then thought of a solution.

62-63. Lord Viṣṇu and Brahmā became a cow and a calf respectively and drank all the nectar in the well. Because of the Lord's illusion, the demons could not forbid the cow and calf. Maya Dānava could understand this.

64. Maya Dānava said to the demons, "What has been destined by the Supreme Lord cannot be undone anywhere, by anyone including the demigods, demons or humans."

devo 'suro naro 'nyo vā neśvaro 'stīha kaścana
ātmano 'nyasya vā diṣṭaṁ daivenāpohituṁ dvayoḥ

Maya Dānava said, "However I plan, you plan or both of us plan, the Lord has planned what is to happen. No one's plan will be successful without His sanction."

65-66. Thereafter, Lord Kṛṣṇa equipped Śiva with all paraphernalia, like a chariot, a charioteer, flag, horses, elephants, bow, shield and arrows, which were empowered by Kṛṣṇa's potency consisting of religion, knowledge, renunciation, opulence, austerity, education and activities. Then Śiva sat on the chariot to fight with the demons.

67-69. Śiva set fire to all three residences and destroyed them. The demigods, saints and others showered flowers and praised Śiva. Śiva became known as Tripurāri.

70. Thus Śrī Kṛṣṇa performed many uncommon, wonderful pastimes, hearing which everyone can be purified.

7.11 The Perfect Society: Four Social Classes

- **1-4:** Yudhiṣṭhira's further inquiries from Nārada Muni
  - Yudhiṣṭira wanted to hear about – Sanātana-dharma and Varṇāśram-dharma
- **5-12:** Nārada Muni explains principles of sanātana dharma
  - 5-7: The eternal religion of all living entities is to satisfy the Supreme Lord Hari
  - 8-11: Thirty qualities by which one can satisfy the Supreme Lord
- **13-24:** The four varṇas or castes
  - 13-16: Occupational duties of the four varṇas
  - 17-20: Emergency duties
  - 21-24: Symptoms of the four varṇas
- **25-29:** Duties of a chaste wife
  - By serving the Vaiṣṇava husband with love and affection, following the footsteps of Lakṣmī, a chaste wife goes to Vaikuṇṭha.
- **30-35:** Duties of the mixed classes and result of occupational duties
  - One should act as per one's nature, and gradually give up those activities. Varṇa is based on one's qualities, not birth.

The first ten chapters of the Seventh Canto described the pure inclination (*ūti*) arising from unalloyed *bhakti* unmixed with material modes. The last five chapters describe the excellence of *varṇāśrama* for material sustenance. They describe *niṣkāma-karma-yoga* as the cause of inclinations for *bhakti* mixed with material modes. In this chapter, Nārada Muni describes the duties of the normal *varṇas*, the duties of women and mixed *varṇas*.

1-4: Yudhiṣṭhira's Further Inquiries From Nārada Muni

1. After hearing about Prahlāda's glorious character adored by great devotees, King Yudhiṣṭhira again inquired from the Nārada Muni with joy.

2. Yudhiṣṭhira wanted to hear about two topics –

Q1. *Sanātana-dharma* or the eternal religion of human beings i.e., *bhakti yoga*

Q2. *Varṇāśrama-dharma* or the social and spiritual duties of humans

Sanātanam means "that which remains after the result is achieved." It refers to *bhakti-yoga* which is not given up even after achieving *prema*.

3-4. Yudhiṣṭhira glorifies Nārada Muni, "Because of your austerities and mystic *yoga*, you are considered as the best of Brahmā's sons. No one knows better than you, all the principles of religious life and how to execute devotional service."

5-12: Nārada Muni Explains Principles of Sanātana Dharma

5. Offering obeisances to Lord Kṛṣṇa, the protector of *dharma* (*dharma-setave*), I will first explain the principles of *sanātana dharma*, which I have heard from Nārāyaṇa.

6. Lord Nārāyaṇa appeared along with Nara in this world, through Mūrti and Dharma. Even now, He is executing austerities at Badarikāśrama.

7. Complete satisfaction by hari-bhakti	
dharma-mūlaṁ hi bhagavān	The Supreme Lord is the root of all religious principles.
sarva-vedamayo hariḥ	Lord Hari is the essence of all Vedic knowledge.
smṛtaṁ ca tad-vidāṁ rājan yena cātmā prasīdati	On the basis of this religious principle, everything is satisfied, O King (This is similar to SB 1.2.6 *sa vai puṁsām... yayātmā su prasīdati*)

The Lord is the cause and the proof (*mūlam*) of *dharma*, since He is the essence of the Vedas. This means that without devotion to Him, *dharma* cannot succeed. Satisfaction doesn't appear by *bhakti* mixed with *karma* as much as it is obtained by pure *bhakti*. And *dharma* without *bhakti* should not be accepted.

Now Nārada answers the first question (Q1 in 7.11.2) of Yudhiṣṭhira on *sanātana dharma*.

8-12: Thirty qualities by which one can satisfy the Supreme Lord	
satyaṁ dayā tapaḥ śaucaṁ	(1) Truthfulness (2) mercy (3) austerity (4) cleanliness
titika īkṣā śamo damaḥ	(5) tolerance (6) discrimination (7-8) mind & sense control
ahiṁsā brahmacaryaṁ ca	(9) nonviolence (10) celibacy

tyāgaḥ svādhyāya ārjavam	(11) charity (12) reading of scripture (13) simplicity
santoṣaḥ samadṛk-sevā	(14) satisfaction (15) serving the equipoised saints
grāmyehoparamaḥ śanaiḥ	(16) gradually taking leave of unnecessary engagements
nṛṇāṁ viparyayehekṣā	(17) observing the futility of unnecessary acts of humanity
maunam ātma-vimarśanam	(18) Silence and gravity (19) researching one's own self
annādyādeḥ saṁvibhāgo bhūtebhyaś ca yathārhataḥ	(20) distributing food equally to all living entities as it is befitting (as much as they deserve)
teṣv ātma-devatā-buddhiḥ sutarāṁ nṛṣu pāṇḍava	(21) seeing every soul as a part of the Supreme Lord, oneself or a devatā
śravaṇaṁ kīrtanaṁ cāsya	(22) hearing about the Lord (23) chanting about Him
smaraṇaṁ mahatāṁ gateḥ	(24) remembering the Lord and His devotees
sevejyāvanatir dāsyaṁ	(25) service (26) worship (27) obeisances, (28) servant
sakhyam ātma-samarpaṇam	(29) becoming a friend (30) surrendering one's whole self.

12. These 30 qualifications must be acquired in the human life. By that one can satisfy the Supreme Personality of Godhead.

The first 21 items in the above list are assistants in *bhakti*. The last 9 items are the core practices of direct devotional service.

Having answered the first question (Q1) of Yudhiṣṭhira about *sanātana-dharma*, Nārada Muni will now answer his second question (Q2) about *varṇāśrama-dharma*. This answer starts from the next verse and continues till the end of the Seventh Canto.

13-24: The Four Varṇas or Castes

13-16: Occupational duties of the four varṇas

13. Dvijas (twice-born) are those who perform the *saṁskāras* (reformatory ceremonies) with *mantras*. Such *brāhmaṇas, kṣatriyas* and *vaiśyas*, purified by family traditions and behavior, should worship the Lord, study the Vedas, give charity and follow the principles of the four *āśramas* [*brahmacarya, gṛhastha, vānaprastha* and *sannyāsa*].

In the *varṇāśrama* system, the first ceremony for purification is *garbhādhāna*, which is performed with *mantras* at the time of sex for propagating a good child. One who uses sex life not for sensual pleasures but only to beget good children is also accepted as a *brahmacārī*. Restraint in sex is possible only when the populace is trained in the above-mentioned thirty qualities (in 7.11.8-11).

14a. Brāhmaṇas have six occupational duties – worshiping Kṛṣṇa and teaching others to worship, studying Vedas and teaching others, accepting charity and giving charity.

14b. Kṣatriyas should not accept charity, but they may perform the other five duties of *brāhmaṇas*. A *kṣatriya* is not allowed to levy taxes on *brāhmaṇas*, but he may make his livelihood by levying taxes and fines upon his other subjects.

15a. Vaiśyas (mercantile community) should follow the directions of *brāhmaṇas* and do agriculture, trade and cow protection.

15b. Śūdras accept a master from a higher social order and serve him to earn livelihood.

16. Four alternative duties for brāhmaṇas (from lowest to highest)

- *i.* *Vārtā* – *Vaiśya's* duty of agriculture, cow protection or trade
- *ii.* *Śālinā* – depending on that which is received without begging
- *iii.* *Yāyāvara* – begging in the paddy field for one day's grains
- *iv.* *Śiloñchanam* – collecting paddy left in a field or in the shops of grain dealers

A *brāhmaṇa* is sometimes offered land and cows in charity, and thus for his livelihood he may act in the same way as a *vaiśya*, by cultivating land, protecting cows and trading off his surpluses. A better process, however, is to pick up grains from a field or shops.

17-20: Emergency duties

17. Emergency situations: Except in emergency, lower persons should not accept the occupational duties of higher castes. In emergency, however, everyone but the *kṣatriya* may accept the means of livelihood of others.

18-20. In emergency, one may accept the following professions

- *i.* *Ṛta* – collecting grains from the field (*uñchaśila*)
- *ii.* *Amṛta* – collecting without begging
- *iii.* *Mṛta* – begging grains
- *iv.* *Pramṛta* – tilling the ground
- *v.* *Satyānṛta* – trade

But one shouldn't accept the profession of dog (*śva-vṛtti*), which is to serve low-grade persons like *śūdras*. *Brāhmaṇas* should be well acquainted with all Vedic knowledge, and *kṣatriyas* should be well acquainted with the worship of demigods.

Brāhmaṇas and *kṣatriyas* should not engage in low service of *śūdras*, because a *brāhmaṇa* is equivalent to the Vedas and a *kṣatriya* is equivalent to the *devatās*. However for *vaiśyas* and *śūdras* to take employment from those lower than themselves is not so faulty.

Kali-yuga is filled with *śūdra* population that has given up the cultivation of spiritual life. This is an emergency situation. Therefore it is now time to train people to become *brāhmaṇas* and take up the work of spiritual progress.

21-24: Symptoms of the four varṇas

21. The symptoms of a brāhmaṇa	
śamo damas tapaḥ śaucaṁ	Mind control, sense control, austerity, cleanliness,
santoṣaḥ kṣāntir ārjavam	satisfaction, forgiveness, simplicity,
jñānaṁ dayācyutātmatvaṁ	knowledge, mercy, complete surrender to Lord Acyuta,
satyaṁ ca brahma-lakṣaṇam	and truthfulness are the symptoms of a *brāhmaṇa*.

Acyutātmatvam: In *varṇāśrama* institution, the symptoms of a *brāhmaṇa*, *kṣatriya*, *vaiśya*, *śūdra*, *brahmacārī*, *gṛhastha*, *vānaprastha*, and *sannyāsī* are all described. The ultimate aim is *acyutātmatvam*—to think always of the Supreme Lord Kṛṣṇa or Viṣṇu. To advance in *bhakti*, one has to become a *brāhmaṇa*, with the above-mentioned symptoms.

22. The symptoms of a kṣatriya	
śauryaṁ vīryaṁ dhṛtis tejas	Bravery in battle, unconquerable, patience, challenging,
tyāgaś cātmajayaḥ kṣamā	charitable, controlling the bodily necessities, forgiving,
brahmaṇyatā prasādaś ca	faithfulness to brahminical principles, always joyful,
satyaṁ ca kṣatra-lakṣaṇam	and truthful—these are the symptoms of the *kṣatriya*.

23. The symptoms of a vaiśya	
deva-gurv-acyute bhaktis	Devotion to demigods, spiritual master and Lord Viṣṇu
tri-varga-paripoṣaṇam	endeavoring for advancement in *dharma*, *artha* and *kāma*,
āstikyam udyamo nityaṁ	believing in the words of spiritual master and scripture,
naipuṇyaṁ vaiśya-lakṣaṇam	expertise in earning money—are the symptoms of *vaiśya*.

24. The symptoms of a śūdra	
śūdrasya sannatiḥ śaucaṁ	Obedience to the higher three castes, cleanliness,
sevā svāminy amāyayā	service to master without duplicity,
amantra-yajño hy asteyaṁ	doing sacrifices without uttering *mantras*, not stealing,
satyaṁ go-vipra-rakṣaṇam	truthfulness and protecting cows and *brāhmaṇas*.

Workers or servants are generally accustomed to stealing. But a first-class servant is one who does not steal. Unless one is pure and has been raised to the standard of a *brāhmaṇa*, *kṣatriya* or *vaiśya*, i.e., a *dvija*, twice-born—the chanting of *mantras* will not be fruitful.

25-29: Duties of a Chaste Wife

25-28. The duties of a chaste wife are –

- To serve the husband with love and affection, according to time and circumstance
- To be favorably disposed toward the husband
- To be equally disposed toward the husband's relatives and friends
- To follow the vows of the husband
- To dress and decorate nicely for husband's pleasure
- To keep the house clean and pure
- To be modest, truthful and attentive
- To control her senses
- To speak sweet words
- Should not be greedy
- Expert in handling household affairs
- Should be fully conversant with religious principles

The basic principle for a chaste woman is to be always favorably disposed toward her husband. When there are no fights between husband and wife, the goddess of fortune Lakṣmī automatically comes home.

29. Result: A woman who serves her husband following the footsteps of Lakṣmī, surely returns back to Godhead, with her devotee husband, and lives happily in Vaikuṇṭha.

A fallen husband is one who is addicted to meat-eating, gambling, intoxication and illicit sex. A chaste wife should not associate with such a fallen husband. Similarly, a husband can separate himself from a woman who is not chaste as per the description of the *śāstra*.

Conclusion: A husband should be a pure Vaiṣṇava and a woman should be a chaste wife with the above qualities. Then both of them will be happy and make spiritual progress. A woman should serve her husband as faithfully as Lakṣmī serves Nārāyaṇa; that is ideal. A man should be an ideal servant of the Lord, and a woman should be an ideal wife like the goddess of fortune.

30-35: Duties of the Mixed Classes and Result of Occupational Duties

Antyaja or mixed classes are those who marry a woman of higher or lower castes. They of two types – (*i*) If a woman of a high caste marries a man of a lower caste, their union is called *pratiloma*. (*ii*) If a woman of a low caste marries a man of a higher caste, their union is called *anuloma*.

The members of such dynasties have their traditional duties as barbers, washermen and so on. Among the *antyajas*, those who are still somewhat pure in that they do not steal and are not addicted to meat-eating, drinking, illicit sex and gambling are called *antevasāyī*.

30. Antevasāyī or *caṇḍālas* (dog-eaters) are not thieves and are not sinful in conduct. They also have their hereditary customs.

31. Acting as per nature: In every *yuga*, an occupation according to one's nature (*svabhāva*) generally brings happiness in this life and after death. This is the opinion of experts in Vedas.

It is better to perform one's own prescribed duty, though inferior, than the duties of others (See *Bhagavad-gīta* 3.35).

According to the symptoms of higher and lower sections of society, there are different varieties of occupational duties. For example, if a tiger kills a man this is not sinful, but if a man kills another man this is sinful. What is a daily affair among the animals is a sinful act in human society. The *antyajas* are accustomed to stealing, drinking and illicit sex, but that is not considered sinful.

32. Result: If one acts according to one's nature and gradually gives up those activities, he gradually attains the *niṣkāma* stage (freedom from material desires) beyond the material modes (*nirguṇatām*).

33-34. Overindulgence as solution: If an agricultural field is cultivated repeatedly, it becomes unsuitable for germinating seeds. Just as drops of ghee on a fire never extinguish the fire but a flood of ghee will, overindulgence in lusty desires mitigates such desires entirely.

Those who are too sinful and have thus been born in the lower classes are allowed to enjoy sinful activities fully, for thus there is a chance that these activities will become detestful to them and they will get the opportunity to be purified.

35. Varṇa is based on qualities, not birth	
yasya yal lakṣaṇaṁ proktaṁ puṁso varṇābhivyañjakam	If one shows the symptoms of being a brāhmaṇa, kṣatriya, vaiśya or śūdra, as described above,
yad anyatrāpi dṛśyeta	even if one is born in a different class,
tat tenaiva vinirdiśet	one should be designated according to those symptoms.

If one who was born in a *brāhmaṇa* family doesn't have brahminical qualifications, he is considered a *brahma-bandhu*. Similarly, if one born in a *śūdra* family acquires the qualities of a *brāhmaṇa*, he should be accepted as a *brāhmaṇa*. Unless one is qualified in terms of the brahminical symptoms, one cannot take *sannyāsa*.

7.12 The Perfect Society: Four Spiritual Classes

1-16: Duties of a Brahmacārī	1-5: General duties of a brahmacārī student living in guru-kula
	6-10: A brahmacārī's conduct and dealings with women
	11-16: Further details of brahmacārī āśrama
17-31: Duties of a Vānaprastha	17: Result of practicing vānaprastha
	18-23: General duties of a vānaprastha
	24-31: Rules for giving up body for a vānaprastha

In 7.11.2, Yudhiṣṭhira asked Nārada Muni about *varṇāśrama*. Nārada described the *varṇas* in 7.11. Now onwards he will describe *āśramas*. In 7.12, Nārada describes the *brahmacārī* and *vānaprastha āśramas*. In 7.13, he describes *sannyāsa āśrama*. In 7.14-15, he describes *gṛhastha āśrama*.

1-16: Duties of a Brahmacārī

1-5: General duties of a brahmacārī student living in guru-kula	
1	• Practicing complete sense control (*dānta*) • Acting only for the benefit of *guru* (*guror hitam*) • Submissiveness to *guru* like a servant (*dāsavan nīco*) • Attitude of firm friendship for the *guru* (*gurau sudṛḍha-sauhṛdaḥ*) *brahmacārī guru-kule vasan dānto guror hitam* *ācaran dāsavan nīco gurau sudṛḍha-sauhṛdaḥ*
2	• Worshiping *guru*, fire, sun and Viṣṇu, early in the morning and the evening (*sandhyas*) while silently and attentively chanting the *gāyatrī mantra*.
3	• Being called by the *guru*, he should study the Vedic mantras regularly. • Daily before and after studies, he should offer respects unto the *guru*'s feet.
4	• Should dress in deerskin garments, a belt of straw, sacred thread, matted locks, and carry a pure *kuśa* grass, a rod, water pot.
5	• Collect alms in the morning and evening and offer it the *guru*. • Eat only if ordered by the *guru*, otherwise fast.

6-10: A brahmacārī's conduct and dealings with women

6. Conduct of a brahmacārī	
suśīlo mita-bhug dakṣaḥ	Well behaved, control on his eating, industrious,
śraddadhāno jitendriyaḥ	faithful to instructions of *guru* and *śāstra*, sense controlled,
yāvad-arthaṁ vyavaharet strīṣu strī-nirjiteṣu ca	interact with women or men controlled by women only as much as necessary

7. Brahmacārī's interactions with women	
varjayet pramadā-gāthām agṛhastho bṛhad-vrataḥ	One who has not accepted the *gṛhastha-āśrama*, must rigidly avoid talking with women or about women,
indriyāṇi pramāthīni	for the senses are so powerful that
haranty api yater manaḥ	they may agitate even the mind of a *sannyāsī*.

Bṛhad-vrata: The word *bṛhad-vrata* refers to a *brahmacārī* who has decided not to marry, and observe strict celibacy, i.e., not to indulge in sex throughout one's life.

8. A young brahmacārī should not allow the young wife of *guru* (if *guru* is married) to care for his hair, massage his body, or bathe him with motherly affection.

There are seven kinds of mothers: one's original mother, wife of *guru*, a *brāhmaṇa*'s wife, king's wife, cow, nurse and earth. Thus the *guru's* wife may care for a disciple like a mother, but if both are young, such a mother cannot touch the *brahmacārī*.

9. Why so much precaution about associating with women?	
nanv agniḥ pramadā nāma	Woman is compared to fire, and
ghṛta-kumbha-samaḥ pumān	man is compared to a butter pot.
sutām api raho jahyād	So, a man should avoid associating even with his own daughter in a secluded place.
anyadā yāvad-artha-kṛt	One should associate with any women only for important business, even if one is not alone.

10. As long as one is not self-realized, he cannot be relieved from bodily conception, which is epitomized by the duality between man and woman. Thus there is every chance of one's fall down due to bewildered intelligence.

11-16: Further details of brahmacārī āśrama

11. Applicable to others also: These principles (described in 7.12.6-10) apply equally to *gṛhasthas* and *sannyāsīs*. The *gṛhastha*, however, is given permission by the *guru* to have sex for procreation.

12. Forbidden items: Those who have taken the vow of celibacy (*bṛhat-vrata*) should not apply ointments, massage the body or head, see a woman, eat meat, drink wine etc.

13-14. Training and graduation: One who is twice-born should reside in the *guru-kula* under the care of *guru* and study the scriptures as per one's ability. The disciple should offer remuneration the *guru* requests, and following the *guru's* order, accept *gṛhastha*, *vānaprastha* or *sannyāsa āśramas* or remain there as a *naiṣṭhika-brahmacārī*.

Studying the scriptures is compulsory for everyone but the *śūdras* and *antyajas*. The scriptures lead one to understand the Absolute Truth—Brahman, Paramātmā or Bhagavān.

It is not compulsory for a *brahmacārī* to become a *gṛhastha*. Because the ultimate aim is to understand the Absolute Truth, there is no necessity of going through all the different *āśramas*. One may proceed to the *sannyāsa-āśrama* directly from the *brahmacārī-āśrama*.

15-16. One should realize the omnipresence of the Supreme Lord in the fire, in the *guru*, in one's self and in all living entities. The Lord is all-pervading, externally and internally as the controller of everything.

16. Result: One can understand the Absolute Truth and attain Him, by practicing in this way, in one of the *āśramas*.

17-31: Duties of a Vānaprastha

17. Result of practicing vānaprastha: By rigidly following the rules of *vānaprastha*, one who has retired from family life, one can easily be elevated to Maharloka.

18-23: General duties of a vānaprastha	
18	• Should not eat grains grown by tilling of the fields. • Should not eat unripe grains that have grown without tilling of the field. • Should not eat grains cooked in fire. • Should eat only fruit ripened by the sunshine.
19	• Should offer in sacrifice cakes made from fruits and grains grown naturally. • Should give up old stock of grains when he obtains some new grains.
20	• Should make a thatched cottage or stay in a cave only to keep the sacred fire. • Should practice enduring snowfall, wind, fire, rain and the heat of the sun.
21	• Should wear matted locks and let his body hair, nails and moustache grow. • Should not cleanse his body of dirt. • Should keep waterpot, deerskin and rod, wear tree bark, and fire-color clothes.
22	• Should remain in forest for 12 years, 8 years, 4 years, 2 years or at least 1 year. • Should not be disturbed by too much austerity.
23	• Should fast when unable to perform prescribed duties due to disease or oldage.

In the previous verse (7.12.23), a *vānaprastha* is recommended to fast when he is unable to perform asuterities. The rest of the chapter describes the actions one should do before fasting. [In the below section "→" indicates "is / are merged into"]

24-31: Rules for giving up body for a vānaprastha

24-25. Merging of the gross body: One should place the fire element in oneself, give up bodily identification and gradually merge the various parts of the gross body into the five material elements which are their sources (causes) as listed below.

- The bodily holes → Sky
- Breathing → Air
- Bodily heat → Fire
- Semen, blood and mucus → Water
- Hard substances like skin, muscle and bone → Earth

The material body is nothing but a combination of the five elements (earth, water, fire, air and sky). Knowledge of this constitutes merging of the body and the five elements. Merging into Brahman in perfect knowledge means understanding perfectly that one is not the body but a spiritual soul.

26-28. Merging of the subtle body

- Object of speech and tongue → Fire
- Craftsmanship and hands → Indra
- Power of movement and legs → Lord Viṣṇu
- Sensual pleasure and genitals → Prajāpati
- Rectum and power of evacuation → Mṛtyu
- Ear and sound vibration→ deities of directions
- Skin and objects of touch → Vāyu
- Eyes and form → Sun
- Tongue and Varuṇa → Water
- Smell and Aśvinī-kumāras → Earth
- Mind and material desires → Moon
- Intelligence and its objects → Brahmā
- False ego (bodily identity) and material activities → Rudra
- Material consciousness and goal of thought → living being/ Vāsudeva
- Demigods and perverted *jīva* → Supreme Being
- Earth → water → fire → air → sky → false ego → *mahat-tattva* (total material energy) → *pradhāna* (unmanifested ingredients) → Supersoul

31. Only the soul remains: When the material body is thus returned to its various material elements, only the indestructible spiritual being remains. He gives up material existence, like fire whose wood has been burned away.

7.13 The Behavior of a Perfect Person

- **1-10:** Qualities of a Sannyāsī
  - 1-3: Conduct of a sannyāsī
  - 4-6: Consciousness of a sannyāsī
  - 7-10: Other qualities of a sannyāsī
- **11-46:** Conversation between prahlāda and an avadhūta brāhmaṇa
  - 11-20: Prahlāda Mahārāja meets a brāhmaṇa and inquires from him
  - 21-23: The brāhmaṇa glorifies Prahlāda Mahārāja
  - 24-34: The brāhmaṇa describes the futility of material happiness
  - 35-37: The two gurus of the brāhmaṇa – bee and python
  - 38-41: Lifestyle of avadhūta brāhmaṇa – habits of eating, dressing, sleeping and travelling
  - 42-46: Giving up the material body and self-realization

In the previous chapter, Nārada Muni described the duties of *brahmacārī* and *vānaprastha*. In this chapter, he describes the conduct of the *sannyāsī* through a conversation between Prahlāda with a renounced person.

1-10: Qualities of a Sannyāsī

1-3: Conduct of a sannyāsī	
1	• Detached, merely keeping the body inhabitable • Not dependent on anything material (*nirapekṣaḥ*) • Travels on earth, passing only one night in a village (*parivrajya*)
2	• If he wears, he wears only a loincloth and an outer covering • When there is no necessity, he should not even accept a *daṇḍa*
3	• Should wander alone (*eka eva cared*) • Should live on alms begged (*bhikṣu*) • Completely satisfied in the self (*ātmārāmo*) • Not dependent on any person or any place (*anapāśrayaḥ*) • A well-wisher to all living beings (*sarva-bhūta-suhṛt*) • Peaceful (*śānto*) • Completely surrendered to Lord Nārāyaṇa (*nārāyaṇa-parāyaṇaḥ*)

4-6: Consciousness of a sannyāsī	
4	• Sees the Supreme Lord (beyond cause and effect) pervading everything • Sees everything (composed of cause and effect) resting on the Supreme Lord
5	• Understands the self during deep sleep, dreaming and waking states • Realizes that bondage and liberation are actually illusory (*māyā-mātraṁ*).
6	• Observes the power of **time**, that causes appearance and disappearance of all beings, instead of praising the uncertain life or death.

7-10: Other qualities of a sannyāsī

7. Teaching and arguments: Literature without spiritual benefit should be rejected. One should not become a professional teacher nor indulge in arguments and take sides.

nāsac-chāstreṣu sajjeta nopajīveta jīvikām
vāda-vādāṁs tyajet tarkān pakṣaṁ kaṁca na saṁśrayet

8a. Disciples: He must not present material allurements to gather many disciples.

8b. Books: He should not read many books or give discourses as a means of livelihood.

8c. Temples: He should not attempt to build many temples or increase material opulence.

The first business of the *sannyāsī* is to preach Kṛṣṇa consciousness, but if, by the grace of Kṛṣṇa, facilities are available, then he may construct temples to give shelter to the serious students of *bhakti*.

9. Paramahaṁsa stage: A spiritually advanced person, who is peaceful and equipoised, does not need to accept the symbols of a *sannyāsī* (like *tridaṇḍa* or *kamaṇḍalu*). As per necessity he sometimes accepts and sometimes rejects them.

10. Evident purpose: Although he may not expose himself, by his behavior his purpose is disclosed. Although he is the greatest orator or poet, he externally presents himself like a dumb man or a child.

Nārada Muni further describes the behavior of such a saintly person by narrating a conversation that happenned between Prahlāda Mahārāja and an *avadhūta brāhmaṇa*.

11-46: Conversation Between Prahlāda and an Avadhūta Brāhmaṇa

11-20: Prahlāda Mahārāja meets a brāhmaṇa and inquires from him

11-13. Sages recite a historical example on this. Once on Sahya Mountain, Prahlāda Mahārāja met a saintly person lying on the ground, covered with dust, feeding himself like a python (*ājagara-vṛtti*). By his activities, bodily features, words, people could not understand whether he was some person they knew.

15. Prahlāda, an advanced devotee, duly worshiped that saintly person touching his feet with head. He then inquired from him very submissively as follows.

Prahlāda studied the bodily features of the saintly person, and understood that he was intelligent and expert, although he was lying down and not doing anything. Prahlāda was naturally inquisitive about why he was lying there inactive.

16-19. Prahlāda asked the saint, "You do not work to earn your livelihood, but you have a stout body, like that of a materialistic enjoyer. You have no money for sense enjoyment. How then has your body become so fat? You appear learned and intelligent, yet you lie down inactive, looking at people doing actions with disgust."

20. Captivated by Prahlāda's sweet words, the saintly person replied with a smile.

21-23: The brāhmaṇa glorifies Prahlāda Mahārāja

21. You have spiritual vision: O best of demons, you are respected by advanced men (*ārya-sattama*). You are aware of the different stages of life and by your inner spiritual vision (*adhyāma-cakṣūṣā*), you can see a man's character and the results of his actions.

In the next verse, the saintly *brāhamṇa* reveals that the cause of Prahlāda's knowledge is his unalloyed *bhakti* (unmixed with fruitive acts or speculative knowledge) towards Kṛṣṇa.

22. Because of your pure devotion (*bhaktyā kevalayā*) to Bhagavān Nārāyaṇa, He is predominant in your heart. He always drives away ignorance, as the sun drives away the darkness of the universe.

23. Although you know everything, you asked some questions. I shall answer you (though I have taken a vow of silence, I shall break it), according to what I have heard from authorities (not concocted), for my self-purification.

24-34: The brāhmaṇa describes the futility of material happiness

24. Desires cause transmigration: Due to insatiable material desires (*tṛṣṇayā*), I was being carried by waves of material nature's laws (*bhava-vāhinyā*), acting in different ways (*karmāṇi*), struggling for existence in various species (*nana-yoniṣu*).

25. Human life is a junction: In the course of such evolution in species by my *karma*, I have attained this human life, which can elevate one to heaven (*svarga*) or liberation (*apavarga*), or degrade one to lower species or rebirth as a human (*tiraścām punar asya*).

Material life is called 'pavarga' because here we are subject to five different states of suffering, represented by the letters *pa, pha, ba, bha* and *ma*.

- *Pa* means *pariśrama* or hard labor
- *Pha* means *phena* or foam from mouth due to labor
- *Ba* means *byarthatā*, disappointment despite hard labor
- *Bha* means *bhaya* or fear due to not knowing what will happen next
- *Ma* means *mṛtyu* or death

One attains 'apavarga' or liberation from the material existence when one attempts to nullify these five different statuses of life (*pavarga*).

26-27. I abandoned material acts because I saw that a man and a woman unite for pleasure in sex, but they actually do not become happy. Material sense enjoyment is simply an imagination. Spiritual happiness is real happiness, and it can be achieved only when one stops all materialistic activities.

tatrāpi dam-patīnāṁ ca sukhāyānyāpanuttaye

karmāṇi kurvatāṁ dṛṣṭvā nivṛtto 'smi viparyayam [26]

One cannot simply cease from materialistic activity and remain inactive for long. One should engage in spiritual activities (according to the orders of Lord Kṛṣṇa), which will solve the problem of suffering.

28. Forgetfulness leads to misery: The conditioned soul forgets his self-interest (his eternal relationship with Kṛṣṇa) due to bodily identification. Attracted by the varieties of the material world, he suffers.

As Kṛṣṇa is always happy, the living entities, who are His parts and parcels, are also happy by nature, but because of being put within this material world and forgetting their eternal relationship with Kṛṣṇa, they suffer.

29-30. Futile search for happiness: Just as a deer cannot see the water within a covered well, but runs after a mirage, the conditioned soul does not see happiness within oneself, but runs for it elsewhere. But because the various material bodies are under the control of material nature, all of one's plans are ultimately baffled.

When one understands one's real identity as a spiritual being, he can understand Kṛṣṇa, the supreme spiritual being, and the real happiness exchanged between Kṛṣṇa and oneself.

31. Futility of enjoyable objects: For a person not free from threefold miseries, who can suddenly die, what is the use of attaining objects of enjoyment with great difficulty?

32-33. A rich man's insecurity: A rich man, who is a victim of senses, is greedy to accumulate wealth, but suffers from insomnia due to fear of government laws, thieves, enemies, family members, animals, beggars, time factor and even his ownself.

34. An intelligent person should give up desire for prestige and money, which is the cause of lamentation, illusion, fear, anger, attachment, poverty, unnecessary labor etc.

śoka-moha-bhaya-krodha- rāga-klaibya-śramādayaḥ
yan-mūlāḥ syur nṛṇāṁ jahyāt spṛhāṁ prāṇārthayor budhaḥ

35-37: The two gurus of the brāhmaṇa

35. The bee and the python are two excellent *gurus* who give us instructions on – satisfaction (*paritoṣam*) and renunciation (*vairāgyam*).

36. The bee teaches detachment from material desires (*virāgaḥ sarva-kāmebhyaḥ*) and accumulating money. Just as the honey accumulated by a bee is taken away by force, anyone can kill a person who own's money and take it away.

37. The python teaches satisfaction (*parituṣṭātmā*), and not desiring to possess more (*anīhaḥ*) but take whatever is achieved in its own way (*yadṛcchopanatād*). If I do not get anything, I am unagitated like a python.

38-41: Lifestyle of avadhūta brāhmaṇa

38. Eating habits: I eat whatever is easily available – small quantity, great quantity, palatable food, stale food, offered with respect, given neglectfully, during the day or night and so on.

39. Dressing habits: I wear whatever is available according to my destiny – linen, silk, cotton, bark or deerskin.

40. Sleeping habits: I lie down wherever possible – on earth, on leaves, grass or stone, on a pile of ashes, or in a palace.

The *brāhmaṇa's* description here indicates different types of births, for one lies down according to one's body. For example, an animal lies down on the ground, and a king or a rich man sleeps in huge palaces.

41. Travels: Sometimes I bathe nicely, decorate with sandalwood pulp, fine garments, garland and ornaments, and travel like a king on an elephant, chariot or horse. Sometimes, however, I travel naked, like a haunted person.

42-46: Giving up the material body and self-realization

42. Avoiding false discrimination and being a well-wisher	
nāhaṁ ninde na ca staumi	I do not praise or criticize people
sva-bhāva-viṣamaṁ janam	who have different mentalities.
eteṣāṁ śreya āśāse	I only desire their welfare, hoping that
utaikātmyaṁ mahātmani	they will agree to become one with the Supersoul.

Good and bad in this world have no meaning because if one is good he may be elevated to higher planets and if one is bad he may be degraded to the lower planets. But this is not the goal of life. Therefore a saintly person does not discriminate between that which is supposedly good and supposedly bad; rather, he desires for everyone to be happy in Kṛṣṇa consciousness, which is the **ultimate goal of life.**

43-44. Fighting false discrimination: Discrimination (*vikalpa*) → consciousness (*citta*) → mind (*manasa*, the root of all acceptance and rejection) → false ego → total material energy (*māyā*)[7]. A thoughtful person should retire from all illusory material activities being situated in self-realization.

45. I have described my history of self-realization to you, O Prahlāda, because you are a self-realized soul and a devotee (*bhagavat-paraḥ*). You do not care for public opinion or so-called scriptures.

46. Prahlāda Mahārāja understood the occupational duties of a *paramahaṁsa*. Prahlāda duly worshiped the saint and departed with his permission.

[7] "→" indicates "should be offered into"

7.14 Ideal Family Life

1-18: Duties of a Gṛhastha	A gṛhastha should offer the results of one's work to Kṛṣṇa and be detached, devoted, neutral, simple, responsible, and maintain others as well.
19-33: The times and places suitable for religious activities	19-26: Kāla – The auspicious times to perform religious acts
	27-33: Deśa – Places suitable for spiritual activities
34-42: Importance of worshipping the deity, brāhmaṇa and Acyuta	34-38: Kṛṣṇa is the Supreme Personality of Godhead and is best receipient of all offerings.
	39-40: Deity worship is introduced for neophyte devotees who cannot properly appreciate other devotees.
	41-42: Brāhmaṇas are the best and are worshiped even by Kṛṣṇa

Having described the three *āśramas* of renunciation, Nārada Muni now explains the path of the householder (*gṛhastha*) engaged in worldly activity according to time and place.

1-18: Duties of a Gṛhastha

1. King Yudhiṣṭhira asked Nārada Muni: "Please explain how we, who are staying at home without knowledge of the goal of life, may also easily attain liberation."

Nārada Muni replied to Mahārāja Yudhiṣṭhira as follows:

2. Dedication to Kṛṣṇa: Householders must act to earn their livelihood, but they should offer the results to Kṛṣṇa and worship great devotees.

3. Hearing about Kṛṣṇa: With faith, one should constantly hear the nectar of Supreme Lord's activities in various incarnations (*avatāra-kathāmṛtam*).

4. Developing detachment: By hearing in good association (*sat-sanga*), one gradually becomes detached from family affection, exactly like a man awakening from a dream.

5. Neutrality and frugality: He should earn only as much as required, should live unattached to family affairs, although externally appearing very much attached.

6. Simplicity and diplomacy: He should keep life simple. He may externally agree to the suggestions of relatives, but internally determined not to create a cumbersome life.

7. Responsibilities and resources: An intelligent householder must perform his daily and occassional duties, by utilizing whatever is created by the Supreme Lord (*acyuta-nirmitam*), and that comes from – (*i*) *divyam* or sky: like rainfall (*ii*) *bhaumam* or earth: like mines and fields and (*iii*) *āntarikṣam* or atmosphere: obtained unexpectedly.

8. Avoiding greed: One may claim proprietorship to as much wealth as required to maintain body and soul together, but one who desires more is a thief (*stena*) and deserves to be punished (*daṇḍam arhati*) by the laws of nature.

9. Equal vision: One should treat animals, birds and flies exactly like one's own sons.

Like children, the unintelligent animals are also sons of the Supreme Lord. Therefore a Kṛṣṇa conscious person should not discriminate between them. Human society should not consider itself the only enjoyer of all the properties of God; animals also have a claim.

10. Don't hanker for tri-vargas: Even if one is a householder, one should not endeavor very hard for *dharma, artha* and *kāma*, and be satisfied with whatever is available with minimum endeavor, according to place and time, by the Lord's grace.

11. Maintaining others: A householder should contribute for the maintenance of even dogs, fallen persons and untouchables. Even one's wife should be engaged in receiving guests.

12. Detachment to wife: One is so possessive about his wife, that he sometimes kills himself, his parents or even *guru* for her sake. If one can give up his attachment to such a wife, he conquers the unconquerable Supreme Lord.

13. By deliberation, one must give up attraction to his wife's insignificant body, which will be ultimately transformed into worms (if buried), stool (if disposed) or ashes (if burned). What value is the wife in comparison to the all-pervading Lord?

kṛmi-viḍ-bhasma-niṣṭhāntaṁ kvedaṁ tucchaṁ kalevaram
kva tadīya-ratir bhāryā kvāyam ātmā nabhaś-chadiḥ

14. One should be satisfied with eating *prasāda* or with performing the *pañca-sūnā* (five kinds of sacrifices). By this, one can give up material attachment and be fixed in the position of a *mahātmā*.

15. Worshiping all: One should worship the demigods, humans, sages, forefathers, living entities and one's self, by the wealth acquired through one's occupation. Thus one is able to worship the Supreme Lord.

16. Performing sacrifices: When one has wealth for gathering all items, one must perform sacrifice according to *śāstric* rules and thus worship the Supreme Lord.

Ultimately all the scriptures are meant to satisfy the Supreme Lord (See BG 3.9). It was possible in Tretā-yuga to perform costly *yajñas*. The same goal can be achieved in Kali-yuga by performing *saṅkīrtana-yajña*, or chanting the holy names of the Lord.

One should also not be too attached to performing sacrifices. Worshiping the *brāhmaṇas* is a greater way of worshiping the Supreme Lord.

17-18. Feeding brāhmaṇas first: Although the Supreme Lord Kṛṣṇa enjoys offerings in sacrificial fire (*agni-mukha*), He is more satisfied when nice food is offered to Him through the mouths of *brāhmaṇas* (*vipra-mukha*). Therefore first offer *prasāda* unto the *brāhmaṇas* and the demigods, and then distribute *prasāda* to other living entities.

19-33: The Times and Places Suitable for Religious Activities

19-26: Kāla – The auspicious times to perform religious acts

19. A rich brāhmaṇa must offer oblations to –

- forefathers – during the dark-moon fortnight in the Bhādra month.
- relatives of forefathers – during the *mahālayā* ceremonies in the Āśvina month.

20-23. One should perform the śrāddha ceremony on the days of *Makara-saṅkrānti, Karkaṭa-saṅkrānti, Meṣa-saṅkrānti, Tulā-saṅkrānti, Akṣaya-tṛtīyā* day, days conjoined with one's own birth star (*janma-nakṣatra*) and so on.

24-26. Benefits of such auspicious times (for any religious activity)

- Brings success in one's short duration of life
- Yields a permanently beneficial result, if one bathes in a sacred river, chants, offers fire sacrifices and worships the Lord at such times
- One flourishes in fruitive activities

27-33: Deśa – Places suitable for spiritual activities

27-29. Religious performances are well executed at places where –

- *Vaiṣṇavas* are available
- Deity of the Supreme Lord is worshiped
- Learned *brāhmaṇas* observe Vedic principles by austerity, education and mercy
- Sacred rivers flow

Anything spiritual done there is certainly very effective.

yatra yatra harer arcā sa deśaḥ śreyasāṁ padam

yatra gaṅgādayo nadyaḥ purāṇeṣu ca viśrutāḥ

Any place where the Deity is worshiped is transcendental; it does not belong to the material world. The forest may be in goodness, the cities and villages in passion, and the brothels, hotels and restaurants in ignorance, but when one lives in the temple community and worships the Deity following the principles, he lives in Vaikuṇṭha.

30-33. Holy places, meant for spiritual advancement

- Sacred lakes like Puṣkara
- Places where devotees live: Kurukṣetra, Gayā, Prayāga, Pulahāśrama, Naimiṣāraṇya, Setubandha, Prabhāsa, Dvārakā, Vārāṇasī, Mathurā, Badarikāśrama, Bindu-sarovara etc.
- Places where Rāma and Sītā stayed: Citrakūṭa, hilly tracts of Mahendra and Malaya.
- Places outside India where Rādhā-Kṛṣṇa Deities are worshiped.

One who desires spiritual advancement may visit these places. Acts performed in these places give a thousand times more result than at other places.

Whenever we perform some religious act, we must do it according to the time (*kāla*), place (*deśa*) and person (*pātra*). Nārada Muni has decribed about *kāla* and *deśa* so far. Now he will describe, to whom everything must be offered.

34-42: Importance of Worshipping Kṛṣṇa, His Deity and Brāhmanas

34. Kṛṣṇa is the best recipient of all offerings: Experts decided that only the Supreme Lord Kṛṣṇa, in whom all that is moving or nonmoving is resting, is the best person to whom everything must be given.

Kṛṣṇa is the root of everything, and therefore He is the best *pātra*, or person, to whom everything must be given (See Bg 5.29 and SB 4.31.14).

35-36. Why only Kṛṣṇa? – At the Rājasūya sacrifice, although many demigods and sages were present, when there was a question of who should be worshiped first, everyone decided that Kṛṣṇa is the most qualified. The entire universe is like a tree, whose root is Kṛṣṇa. Simply by worshiping Him one can worship all living entities.

37-38. Paramātma: The Lord has created many bodies (species) and resides in all of them as the Supersoul. The Supersoul is manifested to the individual soul according to the individual's development of knowledge, austerity and so on.

Gradations of bodily forms: The Supersoul gives intelligence to the individual soul as far as he is able to grasp it (See BG 15.15). Therefore we find the souls in different high and low positions. A living entity with the body of a bird or beast cannot take instructions from the Supreme Soul as adequately as an advanced human being.

39. Deity worship was introduced when great sages saw people disrespectful (*avajña*) to each other (i.e., not respecting the Lord in all beings, specifically other devotees), at the beginning of Tretā-yuga.

40. Neophyte devotees (*prākṛta-bhakta,* or *kaniṣṭha-adhikārī*) faithfully worship the Lord's Deity with all paraphernalia, but are envious of other devotees. The Lord is never satisfied with their service.

For the neophytes who cannot properly appreciate the activities of authorized devotees, Deity worship is the only way for purification and spiritual advancement.

Having described that Lord Kṛṣṇa is the first and best receipent (*su-pātra*) of all offerigs, Nārada Muni will now describe that Kṛṣṇa's devotees are also the best receipents (*su-pātra*).

41. A qualified brāhmaṇa must be accepted as the best in the world. Because of his austerity, Vedic studies and satisfaction, he becomes the counterpart body of the Lord.

A Vaiṣṇava is superior to a brāhmaṇa. A *brāhmaṇa* knows that he is Brahman, but a Vaiṣṇava knows that he is not only Brahman but also an eternal servant of the Supreme Brahman. Therefore, worship of a Vaiṣṇava is superior to worship of the Deity.

42. Even Kṛṣṇa worships the brāhmaṇas who purify the three worlds with their dust and preach the Lord's glories.

nanv asya brāhmaṇā rājan kṛṣṇasya jagad-ātmanaḥ
punantaḥ pāda-rajasā tri-lokīṁ daivataṁ mahat

Reciprocal relationship: The *brāhmaṇas* want to worship Kṛṣṇa, and similarly Kṛṣṇa wants to worship the *brāhmaṇas*. Although a *brāhmaṇa* or Vaiṣṇava is worshiped like the Lord, he remains His faithful servant and never tries to enjoy such prestige.

7.15 Instructions for Civilized Human Beings

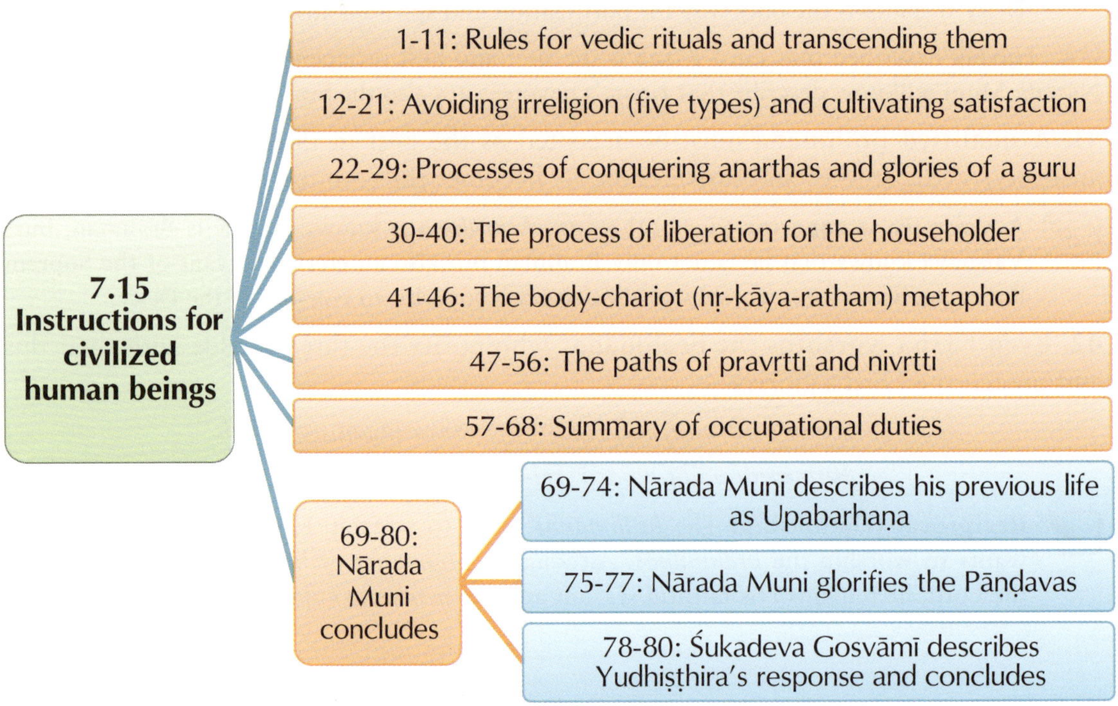

In this chapter, Nārada Muni continues to describe the path of *gṛhasthas* and concludes the discussion with a summary.

In the previous chapter the superiority of the *brāhmaṇa* was described. Now Nārada Muni describes the gradation among the *brāhmaṇas* in different *āśramas*.

1-11: Rules For Vedic Rituals and Transcending Them

1. Gradation of brāhmaṇas

i. **Karma-niṣṭha** – *Gṛhasthas,* who are devoted to performing rituals
ii. **Tapo-niṣṭha** – *Vānaprasthas,* who are devoted to austerity
iii. **Svādhyāya-niṣṭha** – *Brahmacārīs,* who are devoted to studying and preaching Vedas
iv. **Jñāna-niṣṭha** – *Sannyāsīs,* who are devoted to culturing knowledge and *bhakti*

The latter are superior to the former in the list.

2. Whom to give charity? – A person desiring liberation for oneself or one's ancestors, should give charity to a *jñāna-niṣṭha brāhmaṇa* (*sannyāsī*). In his absence, charity may be given to other *brāhmaṇas* like the *karma-niṣṭhas.*

Rules for devotees: Those practicing pure *bhakti* need not perform *karmas* like this, i.e., they need not find a *jñāna-niṣṭha* or a *karma-niṣṭha brāhmaṇa* to give charity. Charity should be given to a devotee of Lord Kṛṣṇa, even if he is not a *brāhmaṇa.* One who desires *mukti* worships *jñānīs*, and one who desires *prema* worships pure devotees.

But gṛhastha devotees still perform these acts of *karma* through appointed representatives, to preserve the normal social standards (Examples: Kings like Bharata and Ambarīṣa).

3. Inviting brāhmaṇas while offering oblations to –

- demigods → invite only two *brāhmaṇas*
- forefathers → invite three *brāhmaṇas*

In either case, only one *brāhmaṇa* will also suffice. Even if one is opulent, he should not endeavor to invite more *brāhmaṇas* or make expensive arrangements.

4. No need to invite more: If one arranges to feed many *brāhmaṇas* during the *śrāddha* ceremony, there will be discrepancies in the time, place, respectability, ingredients etc.

5-6. One should offer prasāda of the Deity (*muni-annam*) to a suitable Vaiṣṇava or *brāhmaṇa*, at an auspicious time and place. This will cause everlasting benefit. One should offer *prasāda* to the demigods, sages, forefathers, relatives and others, seeing them as devotees of the Supreme Lord.

Muni-annam is forest food or food gained by proper means. It should first be offered to Lord Viṣṇu. Then it is given to the Pitṛs and other suitable persons.

7. One should never offer meat, eggs or fish in the *śrāddha* ceremony if he is aware of religious principles (*dharma-tattvavit*). The Lord is pleased with preparations of ghee for the devotees (*muni-anna*), and is not pleased when animals are killed (*paśu-hiṁsayā*).

8. Giving up violence and envy towards all beings by mind, words and body, is the highest *dharma,* for those who desire to advance in superior religion.

naitādṛśaḥ paro dharmo nṛṇāṁ sad-dharmam icchatām
nyāso daṇḍasya bhūteṣu mano-vāk-kāyajasya yaḥ

9. Giving up sacrifices: Persons advanced in knowledge (*jñānīs*) know well about sacrifice (*yajña-vittama*) and are free from material desires (*anīha*). They control the self (*ātma-saṁyamana*), illuminated by spiritual knowledge (*jñāna-dīpite*), and give up sacrifices that result in reactions (*karmamayān yajñān*).

10. The animals become afraid seeing the person doing sacrifice (*dravya-yajña*). They think, "This merciless performer of sacrifices, being ignorant of the purpose of sacrifice and being most satisfied by killing others, will surely kill us."

11. Simple offerings: One, who is actually aware of *dharma* (*dharma-vit*) and is not cruel, should do his daily and occasional duties (*nitya-naimittikīḥ kriyāḥ*) with whatever food is available easily by the grace of the Lord (*daivopapannena*).

12-21: Avoiding Irreligion and Cultivating Satisfaction

12. The knower of *dharma* should avoid five brnches of *adharma* or irreligion.

13-14: Five types of adharma (irreligion)		
i	**Vidharma:** Irreligion	Obstructs the execution of one's own *dharma*, although one considers it *dharma.*
ii	**Para-dharma:** Imitating religion	Introduced by someone else, or performing another person's duties unfit to oneself.
iii	**Ābhāsa-dharma:** Pretentious religion	Whimsically worshiping some demigod by imagination and willfully neglecting one's prescribed duties.
iv	**Upadharma:** Concocted religion	Created by a proud person who opposes Vedic principles, though posing himself as a follower of Vedas.
v	**Chala-dharma:** Cheating religion	Misinterpreting the scriptures by word jugglery.

Any religious principles opposed to the principle of surrendering to the lotus feet of the Supreme Lord, Kṛṣṇa, are to be considered irreligion.

15. Desirelessness: Even a poor man shouldn't strive to improve his economic condition or to become a famous religionist. One who is desireless (*anīha*) also obtains his livelihood without endeavour, just like a python (*ājagara-vṛtti*).

16. Self-satisfaction Vs. Greed	
santuṣṭasya nirīhasya	One who is content, desireless (doesn't strive for livelihood)
svātmārāmasya yat sukham	and satisfied within oneself enjoys divine happiness.
kutas tat kāma-lobhena	Where is such happiness for a lust and greedy person?
dhāvato 'rthehayā diśaḥ	He wanders in all directions desiring to accumulate wealth.

17. Self-satisfied people are most happy	
sadā santuṣṭa-manasaḥ	For one whose mind is always satisfied
sarvāḥ śivamayā diśaḥ	there is happiness everywhere (he has no distress).
śarkarā-kaṇṭakādibhyo	There is no danger even if one walks on pebbles and thorns,
yathopānat-padaḥ śivam	if he has suitable shoes. For him, everything is auspicious.

18. Self-satisfied person Vs. Sense-gratifier	
santuṣṭaḥ kena vā rājan na vartetāpi vāriṇā	O King! Why can't a self-satisfied person be happy with drinking only water?
aupasthya-jaihvya-kārpaṇyād gṛha-pālāyate janaḥ	One who is driven by tongue and genitals, must accept the position of a household dog to satisfy his senses.

Real satisfaction: A devotee is always satisfied as he feels the presence of the Supersoul within his heart and thinks of Him constantly. A devotee is never driven by the dictations of the tongue and genitals, and thus he is never victimized by the laws of material nature.

19. An unsatisfied brāhmaṇa, greedy for senses, gradually loses his spiritual strength, education, austerity, reputation and knowledge.

20. Insatiable greed (cause of dissatisfaction)	
kāmasyāntaṁ hi kṣut-tṛḍbhyāṁ	Needs of hunger and thirst are satisfied when one eats.
krodhasyaitat phalodayāt	Anger is satisfied by chastisement and its reaction.
jano yāti na lobhasya jitvā bhuktvā diśo bhuvaḥ	But one's greed is not satisfied, even by conquering all the directions or enjoying everything in the world.

21. Dissatisfaction leads to fall down: Many scholars, legal advisers, leaders of assemblies fall down into hellish life because of not being satisfied with their positions.

Material greed and spiritual progress: For spiritual advancement, one should be materially satisfied, otherwise, one's greed for material development will result in the frustration of one's spiritual advancement. Good qualifications are lost due to two things: (*i*) poverty and (*ii*) greed. Therefore one should not be so poverty-stricken, but one must try to be satisfied with the bare necessities of life and not be greedy.

Speiritual greed: Greed for propagating *kṛṣṇa-bhakti* and satisfying Kṛṣṇa is spiritual.

Having mentioned about the obstacles (*anarthas*) in spiritual progress, Nārada Muni now explains how to overcome such obstacles.

22-29: Processes of Conquering Anarthas and Glory of Guru

22-25a: How to conquer anarthas		
i	*asaṅkalpāj jayet kāmaṁ*	**Lust** → by being determined not to have sex
ii	*krodhaṁ kāma-vivarjanāt*	**Anger** → by giving up the objective of sense desire
iii	*arthānartheksayā lobhaṁ*	**Greed** → by considering the problems of wealth
iv	*bhayaṁ tattvāvamarśanāt*	**Fear** → by considering that suffering is due to *karma*
v	*ānvīkṣikyā śoka-mohau*	**Lamentation** and **illusion** → by deliberation on the knowledge of matter and spirit
vi	*dambhaṁ mahad-upāsayā*	**Pride** → by serving great devotees
vii	*yogāntarāyān maunena*	**Obstacles in yoga** → by silence
viii	*hiṁsāṁ kāmādy-anīhayā*	**Envy/ Violence** → by giving up sense gratification
ix	*kṛpayā bhūtajaṁ duḥkhaṁ*	**Sufferings from others** → by being merciful to them
x	*daivaṁ jahyāt samādhinā*	**Sufferings from providence** → meditation in trance
xi	*ātmajaṁ yoga-vīryeṇa*	**Sufferings from body** and **mind** → by *haṭha-yoga*
xii	*nidrāṁ sattva-niṣevayā*	**Sleep** → by developing mode of goodness (in eating)
xiii	*rajas tamaś ca sattvena*	**Passion** and **ignorance** → by increasing goodness
xiv	*sattvaṁ copaśamena ca*	**Goodness** → by becoming detached (*śuddha-sattva*)
25b-26: The Importance of guru		
	etat sarvaṁ gurau bhaktyā puruṣo hy añjasā jayet	One can conquer all of these obstacles quickly and easily by service of *guru* with faith and devotion.
	yasya sākṣād bhagavati jñāna-dīpa-prade gurau	The *guru* is as good as the Supreme Lord, because he gives transcendental knowledge for enlightenment.
	martyāsad-dhīḥ śrutaṁ tasya sarvaṁ kuñjara-śaucavat	The knowledge of a person, who thinks that the *guru* is an ordinary mortal, is like elephant bath.

Glory of guru: For the *jñānīs*, destruction of lust and other obstacles is the sought result of devotion to *guru*. For the pure devotees, destruction of lust is a secondary result of devotion to *guru*. If the *guru* is favorably inclined, one receives the Supreme Lord's mercy, and conquers all the influences of the three modes. Otherwise one's study and acquiring knowledge is useless like an elephant bath (an elephant bathes in a lake thoroughly, but as soon as it comes out, it takes dust and strews it over its body).

But the *guru's* relatives and neighbors consider him an ordinary human being! How can a disciple consider him as good as God?

27. Misunderstanding is not factual: Lord Kṛṣṇa is the master of all *jīvas* and material nature (*pradhāna-puruṣeśvaraḥ*). His lotus feet are sought and worshiped by great sages like Vyāsa. Yet, some fools consider Him an ordinary human. (Similarly some think the *guru* an ordinary human, but he is not.)

Guru Vs. God: The *guru* is called *sevaka-bhagavān*, the servitor Personality of Godhead, and Kṛṣṇa is called *sevya-bhagavān*, the Supreme Personality of Godhead who is to be worshiped. The *guru* is the worshiper of God, whereas Kṛṣṇa is the worshipable God.

Non-difference: The Supreme Lord gives real knowledge to the entire world, and the spiritual master, as His representative, carries the message throughout the world. Therefore, on the absolute platform, there is no difference between them.

28. Useless labor: Rituals, regulations and austerities are all meant to control the senses and mind, and come to the point of meditation upon the Supreme Lord. If that end is not achieved, they are simply labor in frustration.

29. Spiritual Vs. material progress: One's occupation, though produces wealth, cannot make one spiritually advanced. Similarly, Vedic rituals done by nondevotees do not bring about attainment of the Lord.

30-40: The Process of Liberation for the Householder

30. To conquer the mind, one must leave the family and live alone independently, by begging as much as he needs, to maintain himself (*sannyāsa*).

This is the process of liberation for the householder. If the householder has association with his family, he cannot conquer lust, though he tries. He should give it up.

31. Āsana: One should do *yoga* in a sacred place, not too high or low, sit comfortably, steady and equipoised, keeping body straight, and chant the Vedic praṇava (*oṁ*).

There is no difference between the Hare Kṛṣṇa *mahā-mantra* and *oṁkāra* because both of them are sound representations of the Supreme Lord Kṛṣṇa (*praṇavaḥ sarva-vedeṣu*). Hare Kṛṣṇa *mantra* may be chanted without consideration of the place, time or the sitting arrangements.

32. Prāṇāyāma: Staring at the tip of the nose, the *yogī* does *pūraka, kumbhaka* and *recaka* (inhaling, exhaling and holding breath), until the mind gives up all desires.

33. Controlling mind: When the mind drifts towards feelings of sense gratification, he should immediately bring it back and arrest it within the core of his heart.

34-35. Peaceful mind: With such practice, in a short time his heart attains peace. When one's consciousness is free from lusty desires, it becomes calm. Then one does not return to materialistic acts.

36. Vāntāśī sannyāsī (vomit eater): One who accepts *sannyāsa* giving up *dharma, artha* and *kāma*, but again returns to such material acts, is called a *vāntāśī*, or a shameless eater of his own vomit.

37. Asattama sannyāsī (great sinner): Sannyāsīs who first consider that the perishable body is not the self, and becomes stool, worms or ashes, but who later think the body is the self, are considered most sinful (*asattamāḥ*).

38-39. Abominable actions in different āśramas		
i	*gṛhasthasya kriyā-tyāgo*	**Gṛhastha** → to give up prescribed duties
ii	*vrata-tyāgo vaṭorapi*	**Brahmacārī** → to give up vows
iii	*tapasvino grāma-sevā*	**Vānaprastha** → to live in village and do social acts
iv	*bhikṣor indriya-lolatā*	**Sannyāsī** → to be addicted to sense gratification
Such lowest renegades and pretenders are bewildered by *māyā*. One should either reject them, or if possible, compassionately teach them to resume their position.		

The next verse criticizes a fallen *sannyāsī* who is described above.

40. The human form is meant for understanding the self and the Supreme Self. If one (specifically a *sannyāsī*) understands them, by being purified by advanced knowledge, why should he strive to maintain the body for sense gratification?

The material body is the cause of bondage for a person bewildered by *māyā*. But for an attentive spiritual seeker, the same body is the cause of liberation. Thus the human body may be used in two ways – to degrade to hellish conditions or to go back to Godhead. This meaning is conveyed through the metaphor of body-chariot with the soul as the passenger. If one drives this chariot well with the directions of a bona fide *guru*, one can reach the destination, i.e., one goes back to Godhead. But if one drives it whimsically, one may have an accident, i.e., one returns to the cycle of birth and death. This is now described in the next six verses.

41-46: The Body-Chariot (nṛ-kāya-ratham) Metaphor		
41	Horses	Senses
	Reins	Mind (master of senses)
	Destinations	Sense objects
	Chariot driver	Intelligence
	Seat of the charioteer	Consciousness
42	Spokes of wheels	Ten life airs
	Wheels	Religion and irreligion
	Passenger	Conditioned soul
	Bow	Praṇava *oṁkāra* (obtained by *guru's* mercy)
	Arrow	Pure soul
	Target	Supreme Lord Viṣṇu or Kṛṣṇa[8] (goal of life)
43-44	Enemies (to be conquered to progress towards the target)	Attachment, greed, lamentation, illusion, fear, madness, false prestige, envy, bewilderment etc (influenced by passion and ignorance and sometimes by goodness also)
45	Sword to destroy the enemies	Knowledge sharpened by service to *guru* and *paramparā,* and the Lord's mercy (*acyuta-bala*). Thus, one is attains spiritual bliss and gives up material body (chariot).
46	Wrong path	Not taking shelter of Acyuta and Baladeva, the soul comes to the path of sense enjoyment in this world.
	Dark well	*Saṁsāra*: Being thrown into material existence.
	Plunderers	Attraction and repulsion to sense objects

---

[8] **Viṣṇu is the goal:** As an arrow is aimed with a bow and shot at a target/ enemy, the *jīva* is shot at the Lord by uttering *oṁ*. But that does it mean that the Lord is the enemy? No! It means that Lord Viṣṇu is the goal of one's life, and a devotee takes the arrow of his purified life, and with the bow—the transcendental chanting of *praṇava*, or the Hare Kṛṣṇa *mantra*—he throws himself toward the Supreme Lord Viṣṇu or Kṛṣṇa. It is like Arjuna's aiming the fish in the wheel at Draupadī's *svayamvara*. Just as Arjuna pierced the target with an arrow by the strength of his arms and attained Draupadī, the devotees attain the Lord by the strength of their *bhakti*.

Even if one considers the Lord as enemy, and thus constantly thinks of him, one is purified and attains liberation (as described in Chapter One).

Some devotees are in vīra-rasa (chivalrous mood) with the Lord, who becomes their so-called enemy. For example, Bhīṣma pierced Kṛṣṇa's body in Kurukṣetra with arrows. Similarly, if with the arrow of chanting Lord's holy name, one pierces His lotus feet, one goes back to Godhead.

If enjoyment in the world is a wrong path that binds one to the material existence, why is it prescribed in the scriptures? – Different prescriptions are given according to one's qualification. By the path of *pravṛtti* one remains a householder. By the path of *nivṛtti* one becomes a *sannyāsī*. This is explained in the next ten verses.

47-56: The Paths of Pravṛtti and Nivṛtti

47. Two Vedic paths – Pravṛtti and Nivṛtti	
pravṛttaṁ ca nivṛttaṁ ca dvi-vidhaṁ karma vaidikam	According to the Vedas, there are two kinds of activities—*pravṛtti* and *nivṛtti*.
āvartate pravṛttena	*Pravṛtti* means raising from a lower to a higher status of material life, by which one is entangled.
nivṛttenāśnute 'mṛtam	*Nivṛtti* means the cessation of material desire by which one is purified and becomes fit for eternal, blissful life.

48-51: Pravṛtti mārga – Path of enjoyment

48-49. Pravrtti activities are meant for the fulfillment of one's material desires. They include different rituals, animal sacrifices and public welfare activities.

50-51. Pitṛ-yāna: Through the celestial smoke from the sacrifices, the *jīva* attains the moon planet. After enjoying, he again descends to earth through rain, to become herbs, which are eaten by people and will turn into semen. Thus he is reborn.

53-55: Nivṛtti mārga – Path of detachment

52-53. Giving up sacrifices: The *brāhmaṇa*, purified by *saṁskāras* (from impregnation to death), offers his sensual actions into the senses illuminated by the fire of knowledge: Actions → senses → mind → speech → syllables → *oṁ* → *bindu* → *nāda* (vibration of sound) → *prāṇa* (life air) → *mahati* (the Supreme). ["→" denotes "are offered into"]

If we simply place ourselves at Kṛṣṇa's lotus feet by chanting the Hare Kṛṣṇa *mantra*, we need not take much trouble in arranging to return to the spiritual world. By the mercy of Śrī Caitanya Mahāprabhu, this is very easy.

54-55. Deva-yāna: On his path of ascent, the progressive living entity successively enters the plantes of the fire, the sun and finally Brahmāloka. He then surpasses his gross, subtle and causal designations and attains his pure spiritual state as soul and doesn't return to the material world.

56. Conclusion: One who is fully aware of the paths of *pitṛ-yāna* and *deva-yāna* through the eyes of scriptures, is never bewildered, though situated in a material body.

57-68: Summary of Occupational Duties

57. The all-pervading and ever-existing Supreme Brahman	
ādāv ante janānāṁ sad	He always exists in the beginning and in the ending of everything and all living entities,
bahir antaḥ parāvaram	internally and externally, as superior and inferior objects,
jñānaṁ jñeyaṁ vaco vācyaṁ	as the knowledge (or senses), knowable (or sense objects), as expression of words, the object of understanding,
tamo jyotis tv ayaṁ svayam	as darkness and light. He is personally everything.

This verse explains the Vedic aphorism, *sarvaṁ khalv idaṁ brahma:* Everything that exists is indeed Brahman or the Supreme Lord. It is also explained in the *catuḥ-ślokī Bhāgavatam* (SB 2.9.33-36) that the Lord existed even before the creation.

How can the *sannyāsī* say that everything is the Supreme Lord or Brahman, when everyone perceives difference between enjoyed objects and enjoyers?

58. The world is real, not false: Although one may consider the sun's reflection from a mirror to be false, sunlight has its factual existence (without the sunlight the reflection would be impossible). Similarly, one cannot prove by speculation that there is no reality.

Reality behind the reflection: The impersonalists try to prove that the varieties we see in this world are false (*vivarta-vāda*), just as a rope seen to be a snake is false. But the Vaiṣṇavas say that although the idea that the rope is a snake is false, the snake exists in reality. The varieties of this world (although temporary) would be impossible unless there were a real prototype in the spiritual world.

59. Body is false (temporary): The body is neither a combination nor transformation of the five material elements. Because the body and its ingredients are neither distinct nor amalgamated, all such theories are insubstantial.

Lord Kṛṣṇa and His multi-energies exist simultaneously. Everything is an expansion of Kṛṣṇa's energy. So, He is simultaneously one with and different from everything. Yet, by worshiping stone or wood we get no result, but when the stone and wood are represented in the Lord's original form as a Deity, by worshiping the Deity we get the desired result.

60. World is false (temporary): Body cannot exist without subtle sense objects. Since the body is temporary, the sense objects are also naturally false or temporary.

If the body and the world are false, how does the perception that elements are real arise?

61. Dualities are due to illusion: When a substance and its parts are separated, seeing similarity between them is illusion (*bhrama*). The prescriptions and prohibitions in scriptures are like wakeful and sleep states in a dream.

The temporary or unreal material world is a reflection of the eternal real spiritual world. Material body is false or temporary but the Supreme Lord's spiritual body is eternal.

Although the water in a mirage is false, but water exists outside the desert. Similarly, nothing real (permanent) is in this material world, but reality is in the spiritual world. The Lord's form and His abode (Goloka and Vaikuṇṭha) are eternal realities.

62-65: Philosophy of Adviata (three types of oneness)

62. One realizes the self and gives up the three states of wakefulness, dreaming and sleep, contemplating on the following three types of oneness or non-difference (*advaita*).

63. Bhāvādvaitaṁ (oneness of conceptions) means seeing the effect and the cause as one (*kārya-kāraṇa-vastv-aikya*), like threads (cause) being related to a cloth (effect). That duality is ultimately unreal.

64. Kriyādvaitaṁ (oneness of activities) is attained when one dedicates all activities done with body, mind and words directly to the service of the Supreme Lord (*sarva-karma-samarpaṇam*).[9]

65. Dravyādvaitaṁ (oneness of objects or interest) is attained when the ultimate goal[10] (*svārtha-kāmayor*) of one's self, wife, children, relatives and all other embodied living beings is one.

66. Summary of the conduct of āśramas: In the absence of danger, one must perform perform his prescribed duties according to his status of life, with the things, endeavors, process and place that are not forbidden for him, and not by any other means.

67. Conclusion: When one does occupational duties according to these instructions, and worships Kṛṣṇa, one can attain Kṛṣṇa even while remaining at home.

Previously Yudhiṣṭhira had said (in 7.14.1) that he was a householder ignorant of spiritual life. But one should not think that the Pāṇḍavas are amongst the regular householders. Nārada Muni encouraged Yudhiṣṭhira by saying, "You are already on the safe side because you, along with your entire family, have become a pure devotee of Kṛṣṇa."

68. Kṛṣṇa's grace on the Pāṇḍavas: O Yudhiṣṭhira, by serving Kṛṣṇa's lotus feet, all of you have excaped great dangers, conquered great enemies and gathered ingriedients for sacrifices. By His grace, may you be delivered from material involvement.

---

[9] One must be guided by the *guru* on this oneness; one should not manufacture one's own oneness.

[10] The actual interest of all living entities is to go back to Godhead.

Bhagavān Kṛṣṇa, the common goal of all *āśramas,* as explained in the last five chapters, is the goal of pure devotees, both *sādhaka* and *siddha*. However, He throws the *siddhas* into the whirlpool of both bliss and danger to make them dance in the waves of His love.

The Pāṇḍavas are a practical example of how to live in security and safety by the grace of Kṛṣṇa. Everyone should follow the example of the Pāṇḍavas.

69-80: Nārada Muni Concludes

69-74: Nārada Muni describes his previous life as Upabarhaṇa

69. In another Mahā-kalpa, I was a respectable Gandharva known as Upabarhaṇa.

70. Position: I was beautiful, friendly and had a well-built attractive body, pleasing to women. Thus I was bewildered, always feeling lusty desires.

71. Festival: Once the Gandharvas and Apsarās were invited by the prajāpatis to take part in a *saṅkīrtana* festival to glorify the Supreme Lord, in the assembly of demigods.

72. Offense: I, surrounded by women, went there and sang the glories of other demigods in an intoxicated way. The Prajāpatis cursed me, "Because you transgressed etiquette, become a *śūdra*, devoid of beauty."

73. Reaction: I took birth as a *sūdra*, son of a maidservant, and engaged in the service of Vaiṣṇavas. Consequently, in the next life, I took birth as the son of Lord Brahmā.

74. Conclusion: I have thus described to you the *dharma* of a *gṛhastha*, which destroys sin. The process of chanting the Lord's holy name is so powerful that it enables even *gṛhasthas* to easily gain the ultimate result achieved by *sannyāsīs*.

75-77: Nārada Muni glorifies the Pāṇḍavas

75. You Pāṇḍavas are most fortunate, for Kṛṣṇa, the Supreme Brahman, personally lives in your palace, because He is attracted to you. Knowing this great saints visit your house. (This verse is same as 7.10.48)

76. Kṛṣṇa acts as your well-wisher, friend, cousin, heart and soul, worshipable director and *guru*, although He is sought by great sages, who seek liberation and bliss.

After instructing Yudhiṣṭhira, Nārada Muni prays for Lord Kṛṣṇa's blessings so that He will be pleased and that everyone becomes perfect in God consciousness and go back to Him.

77. Nārada Muni's final prayer	
na yasya sākṣād bhava-padmajādibhī	Even Śiva and Brahmā cannot understand Him
rūpaṁ dhiyā vastutayopavarṇitam	or describe His true form by their intelligence.

maunena bhaktyopaśamena pūjitaḥ	He is worshiped by silence, by cessation of material activities and by devotional service.
prasīdatām eṣa sa sātvatāṁ patiḥ	May that master of devotees be pleased with us.

78-80: Śukadeva Gosvāmī describes Yudhiṣṭhira's response and concludes

78. Hearing Nārada Muni's instructions, Yudhiṣṭhira Mahārāja felt great pleasure, and in great ecstasy, love and affection, he worshiped Lord Kṛṣṇa (and Nārada Muni).

79. Nārada Muni bade them farewell and departed. Yudhiṣṭhira Mahārāja was struck with wonder having heard that Kṛṣṇa, his cousin was the Supreme Lord.

80. All the living entities were generated from the daughters of Dakṣa. I have now described them and their different dynasties.

SPECIAL VERSES

1. Vaiṣṇava Compassion

naivodvije para duratyaya-vaitaraṇyās
tvad-vīrya-gāyana-mahāmṛta-magna-cittaḥ
śoce tato vimukha-cetasa indriyārtha-
māyā-sukhāya bharam udvahato vimūḍhān

"O best of the great personalities, I am not at all afraid of material existence, for wherever I stay I am fully absorbed in thoughts of Your glories and activities. My concern is only for the fools and rascals who are making elaborate plans for material happiness and maintaining their families, societies and countries. I am simply concerned with love for them." (7.9.43: Prayer by Prahlāda Mahārāja)

- **Place of misery:** The material world is *duḥkhālayam aśāśvatam* [BG 8.15]—temporary and miserable—cannot be turn into into *sukhālayam*, a place of happiness, as material nature works in her own way. Everyone struggles very hard to fight through the modes of passion and ignorance and conquer material nature, but at the end everyone is vanquished by nature's laws. (7.9.43 P)
- **Lord's mercy is the only hope:** To cross Vaitaraṇī between the material and spiritual worlds, is an extremely difficult task. BG 7.14: *daivī hy eṣā guṇa-mayī mama māyā duratyayā*. Therefore one cannot surpass the stringent laws of material nature except by the mercy of the Supreme Lord. (7.9.43 P)
- **Prakṛti fools the materialist:** The materialists make elaborate political, social and cultural plans to adjust the material miseries, but their attempts to become happy are repeatedly baffled. They try to create a comfortable situation, but only succeed in creating another uncomfortable situation. This situation is called *māyā-sukhāya* or temporary materialistic happiness. (7.9.43 P)

- **Who is happy?:** Those who are trying to serve the Lord are happy, whereas those who have no assets in Kṛṣṇa consciousness and are struggling for existence are not only foolish but extremely unhappy also. (7.9.43 P)
- **Vaiṣṇava compassion:** A devotee laments to see others bereft of love of God, rotting in material activities for transient material pleasure and spoiling their lives toiling all day and night simply for sense gratification. So a devotee devises various plans to deliver them from the clutches of *māyā*. A devotee may even go to hell to deliver the conditioned souls.
- **Goṣṭhy-ānandī** wants to see everyone taking advantage of the holy name of the Lord and advance in spiritual life. Prahlāda Mahārāja is an outstanding example of the same. (CC Adi 7.92 P)
- **Māyā-sukha Vs. real sukha:** Goddess Durgā provides temporary benefits to her worshipers, which result only in *māyā-sukha* (illusory happiness); such happiness does not endure. On the other hand, the extraordinary material opulences received by devotees like Prahlāda and Dhruva were not *māyā-sukha*, but were direct gifts of the goddess of fortune, who resides in the heart of Nārāyaṇa. (5.18.22 P)
- **Who is assured of protection?:** A devotee engaged in the Lord's service, may not be expert in self-defense, but because of being fully dependent on the lotus feet of the Supreme Lord, he is always sure of protection by Him. (9.4.28 P)
- **Art of Kṛṣṇa consciousness:** Bhaktivinoda Ṭhākura, Dhruva Mahārāja and Prahlāda Mahārāja were *gṛhasthas*, householders, but they trained themselves and learned the art of always remaining in Kṛṣṇa consciousness, with no interruption in their service. "What is that art?" – *tvad-vīrya-gāyana-mahāmṛta-magna-cittaḥ*: simply glorifying the victorious activities and pastimes of the Lord. (Science of Self Realization book)
- **Healthy fear:** Prahlāda Mahārāja did not fear the material existence because of his full absorption in the Lord. But he was afraid of the bad association in *saṁsāra* which was filled with hatred and criticism towards the Lord.

2. The Basis of Caste

yasya yal lakṣaṇaṁ proktaṁ
puṁso varṇābhivyañjakam
yad anyatrāpi dṛśyeta
tat tenaiva vinirdiśet

"If one shows the symptoms (*yasya yal lakṣaṇaṁ*) of being a *brāhmaṇa, kṣatriya, vaiśya* or *śūdra* (*varṇābhivyañjakam*), as described (*proktaṁ*), even if he has appeared in a different class (*yad anyatrāpi dṛśyeta*), he should be accepted according to those symptoms of classification (*tat tenaiva vinirdiśet*)." (7.11.35)

Context: Mahārāja Yudhiṣṭhira inquires from Nārada Muni about the actual religion of a human being and about the special characteristics of *varṇāśrama-dharma*, which marks the highest status of human civilization. Nārada Muni speaks this verse in relation to the identification of the four social orders.

- **The tendency** of a particular man towards work is determined by the modes of material nature which he has acquired (BG 4.13 P).
- **Prescribed duties** are duties enjoined according to one's psychophysical condition, under the spell of the modes of material nature. (BG 3.35 P)
- **One cannot suddenly give** up a profession to which he is accustomed (conditioned). So, it is recommended that one should not give it up haphazardly, but try to be gradually awakened. (7.11 Summary)
- **Lord Kṛṣṇa has created** the four *varṇas* for the systematic development of Kṛṣṇa consciousness. (BG 4.13)
- **Perfect education:** The spiritual master should be expert enough to recognize the tendencies of the student and immediately train him in that line. This is perfect education. One should be selected for training according to his qualifications.
- **Saves time:** Training everyone in everything is waste of time. If one is inclined toward production, business or agriculture, he should be trained in those fields. If

one is philosophical, he should be trained as a philosopher. If one is militaristic, he should be trained as a warrior. And if one has ordinary ability, he should remain a laborer.

- **Example:** Arjuna belonged to a *kṣatriya* family. He and his brothers were never trained as philosophers. Droṇācārya was their master and teacher, and although he was a *brāhmaṇa*, he taught them Dhanur Veda [military science], not *brahma-vidyā* (theistic philosophy).

- **Following another's path**
  - **Lord Kṛṣṇa says,** "It is far better to discharge one's prescribed duties, even though faultily, than another's duties perfectly." (BG 3.35)
  - **Social order will be disrupted** if the unqualified *śūdras* become so-called *brāhmaṇas* and *kṣatriyas*. (9.16.28 P)
- **Exceptions**
  - As Kṛṣṇa is transcendental to this system of four castes, a person in Kṛṣṇa consciousness is also transcendental to all divisions of human society. (BG 4.13 P)
  - Although Paraśurāma belonged to the brahminical group, he circumstantially had to work as a *kṣatriya*.
  - Viśvāmitra was born in a *kṣatriya* family, by austerities and penances he achieved the position of a *brāhmaṇa*.
  - These histories confirm the statements in *śāstra* that a *brāhmaṇa* may become a *kṣatriya*, a *kṣatriya* may become a *brāhmaṇa* or *vaiśya*, and a *vaiśya* may become a *brāhmaṇa*, by achieving the required qualities. (9.16.28 P)
- **Other sources with similar verse**
  - *cātur-varṇyaṁ mayā sṛṣṭaṁ guṇa-karma-vibhāgaśaḥ* (BG 4.13).
  - *sthito brāhmaṇa-dharmeṇa brāhmaṇyam....* (Mahābhārata Anuśāsana-parva, Chapter 163)
  - Śrīla Śrīdhara Svāmī comments: *śamādibhir eva brāhmaṇādi-vyavahāro mukhyaḥ...* (CC Madhya 24.330)
  - *śūdre tu yad bhavel lakṣma dvije tac ca na vidyate...* (Mahābhārata Vana-parva, 177.20)
  - *śūdra-yonau hi jātasya sad-guṇānupatiṣṭhataḥ...* (Mahābhārata Vana-parva, Chapter 203.11-12)

3. Nine Processes of Bhakti

śrī-prahrāda uvāca
śravaṇaṁ kīrtanaṁ viṣṇoḥ smaraṇaṁ pāda-sevanam
arcanaṁ vandanaṁ dāsyaṁ sakhyam ātma-nivedanam
iti puṁsārpitā viṣṇau bhaktiś cen nava-lakṣaṇā
kriyeta bhagavaty addhā tan manye 'dhītam uttamam

Prahlāda Mahārāja said: Hearing and chanting about the transcendental holy name, form, qualities, paraphernalia and pastimes of Lord Viṣṇu, remembering them, serving the lotus feet of the Lord, offering the Lord respectful worship with sixteen types of paraphernalia, offering prayers to the Lord, becoming His servant, considering the Lord one's best friend, and surrendering everything unto Him (in other words, serving Him with the body, mind and words)—these nine processes are accepted as pure devotional service. One who has dedicated his life to the service of Kṛṣṇa through these nine methods should be understood to be the most learned person, for he has acquired complete knowledge. (7.5.23-24)

The following verse by Śrīla Rupa Gosvāmī presents the names of great devotees who exemplified the nine processes of *bhakti* described by Prahlāda in the above verse.

śrī-viṣṇoḥ śravaṇe parīkṣid abhavad vaiyāsakiḥ kīrtane
prahlādaḥ smaraṇe tad-aṅghri-bhajane lakṣmīḥ pṛthuḥ pūjane
akrūras tv abhivandane kapi-patir dāsye 'tha sakhye 'rjunaḥ
sarvasvātma-nivedane balir abhūt kṛṣṇāptir eṣāṁ param

"Parīkṣit Mahārāja attained salvation simply by hearing, and Śukadeva Gosvāmī attained salvation simply by chanting. Prahlāda Mahārāja attained salvation by remembering the Lord. The goddess of fortune, Lakṣmīdevī, attained perfection by worshiping the Lord's lotus feet. Pṛthu Mahārāja attained salvation by worshiping the Deity of the Lord. Akrūra attained salvation by offering prayers, Hanumān by rendering service, Arjuna by establishing friendship with the Lord, and Bali Mahārāja by offering everything to the service of the Lord."

THEMATIC COMPILATIONS

1. Glories of Bhakti-yoga

Bhakti or devotional service unto Lord Śrī Kṛṣṇa is the eternal constitutional position of every living entity. However, one who conditioned in this world is forgetful of his original position and is swayed away by the waves of material nature. *Guru, sādhu* and *śāstra* together make an unpretentious attempt to remind the conditioned soul of his eternal relationship with Kṛṣṇa and delineate the process of reviving it to attain the ultimate goal of life, *kṛṣṇa-prema* or love of Godhead. *Śrīmad-Bhāgavatam* repeatedly recommends and glorifies the process of *bhakti-yoga* as the topmost means for the spiritual upliftment of the humanity. The following are the various glories of *bhakti-yoga* mentioned in Canto Seven, categorized in relevant sections.

Bhakti manifests all good qualities in a person

1. A Vaiṣṇava is automatically a *brāhmaṇa*. One may be a demon by birth, yet by practicing *bhakti,* he can possess all the qualities of a perfect *brāhmaṇa.* (7.4.31-33 *brahmaṇyaḥ śīla-sampannaḥ...*)
2. All good qualities which exist in the Lord, also exist forever in His devotees. And such devotees are glorified even in demoniac assemblies. (7.4.34-35)
3. A devotee is so humble that even if he is fully qualified, he feels himself disqualified even to offer prayers to Lord. (7.9.8 *brahmādayaḥ sura-gaṇā...*)
4. *Bhakti* or Kṛṣṇa consciousness is the only means to make everyone fearless. (7.9.5)

Bhakti awards liberation

5. *Bhakti* is the only way to be freed from all material contamination. (7.5.32 *naiṣāṁ matis tāvad urukramāṅghriṁ...*)
6. By performing various activities of *bhakti* one becomes free from all material contamination and attains the platform of loving service to the Lord. (7.7.30-33 *guru-śuśrūṣayā bhaktyā...,* 7.7.37)
7. Anyone can be purified of material life if he offers prayers to the Lord and hears the Lord's glories. (7.9.12 *pūyeta yena hi pumān anuvarṇitena*)
8. Shelter of the Lord's lotus feet is the ultimate goal for liberation from conditional life. (7.9.16 *trasto 'smy ahaṁ kṛpaṇa-vatsala...*)

Bhakti is our natural function

9. Attraction towards Kṛṣṇa is natural for all living entities. (7.5.14)
10. Viṣṇu is the center of love for everyone, and therefore to engage in the loving service of the Lord is natural. (7.6.2)
11. The Lord is naturally the master of all, and we are naturally His servants. (7.10.6)
12. Since the Lord is intimately related to us, there are no impediments in pleasing Him. (7.6.19)

Bhakti is the most recommended path

13. To give up embarrassment by material sufferings, one must take full shelter of Lord Kṛṣṇa. (7.5.5 *tat sādhu manye...*)
14. *Bhakti* should be practiced from childhood. (7.6.1 *kaumāra ācaret prājño...*)
15. Perfection of human form is attained by engaging in *bhakti*. (7.6.1)
16. One can show mercy to all living entities by enlightening them in *bhakti*. (7.6.24)
17. The best of all activities is that which develops one's love for God. (7.7.29)
18. *Bhakti* is the ultimate goal of human life. (7.7.55 *etāvān eva loke 'smin...*)
19. The only remedy to get out of miserable life is to engage in the Lord's service. (7.9.17 *yasmāt priyāpriya-viyoga...*). No remedy is successful without the Lord's shelter. (7.9.19 *bālasya neha śaraṇaṁ pitarau nṛsiṁha...*)
20. One can cross the ocean of nescience by glorifying the Lord. (7.9.18 *so 'haṁ priyasya suhṛdaḥ paradevatāyā...*)
21. Vedas, scriptures, religion or everyone's occupational duty, all of them must aim at understanding Kṛṣṇa, the Supreme Lord. (7.11.7 *dharma-mūlaṁ hi bhagavān...*)

No barriers in transmitting bhakti

22. *Bhakti* is uninterrupted and can be transmitted in any circumstances. Prahlāda Mahārāja received it in womb of his mother. (7.7.16-17)
23. A pure devotee brings transformation even in demons. Prahlāda Mahārāja preached Kṛṣṇa consciousness to his schoolmates. (7.8.1-2)

Kṛṣṇa is pleased by bhakti alone

24. Qualities that can satisfy the Supreme Lord. (7.11.8-12)
25. Only bhakti can satisfy Lord, e.g. Gajendra (7.9.9 *manye dhanābhijana...*)

Bhakti bestows all benedictions

26. Nothing is unobtainable for devotees who satisfy the Supreme Lord. (7.6.25)
27. By devotional service one achieves what is obtainable by the *paramahaṁsa*. (7.9.50)

Result of absorption in Kṛṣṇa

28. Somehow or the other, if one is absorbed in Kṛṣṇa (even with a negative emotion), one gets liberated. (SB 7.1.26, 30-32, 47 *tasmād vairānubandhena...*)

Attitude and vision of great bhaktas

29. One who follows nine processes of *bhakti* should be understood to be the most learned person. (7.5.23-24 *śravaṇaṁ kīrtanaṁ viṣṇoḥ...*)
30. Devotees do not see any living entity as an enemy or friend but think everyone as an eternal servant of God. (7.5.11-12)
31. Unlike the pseudo spiritualists who are interested in their own deliverance, the devotees are concerned to bring people to shelter of the Supreme Lord. (7.9.43-46)
32. A devotee doesn't want any material possession but only service to a devotee. (7.9.24 *tasmād amūs tanu-bhṛtām aham āśiṣo 'jña...*)
33. A pure devotee is always grateful and aspires to serve one's spiritual master. (7.9.28)
34. A pure devotee doenst desire any material benefit from the Lord and rejects whatever hampers their devotional service. (7.9.55, 7.10.1-2)
35. Wherever exalted devotees stay, that place and the dynasties there, even if condemned, are purified. (7.10.19 *yatra yatra ca mad-bhaktāḥ...*)

The Lord's reciprocation with the devotees

36. The Supreme Lord protects a devotee in all conditions. (7.5.41)
37. Bodily needs are automatically fulfilled for a person absorbed in *bhakti*, like a small child cared by his mother doesn't know how his bodily needs are fulfilled. (7.4.38)
38. The Lord proves His devotee's words true. (7.8.17 *satyaṁ vidhātuṁ nija-bhṛtya...*)
39. Pure devotees of the Lord are sent by Him to teach the mankind. (7.10.3)
40. The Lord never induces His devotees to do something unbeneficial. (7.10.4)
41. As one surrenders to the Lord, He rewards him accordingly. (7.9.27)
42. When the Lord is pleased with the living entity because of his devotional service, one develops an equal vision towards all. (7.5.12)
43. The Lord's chastising a demon and accepting a devotee's prayers - are equally glorious, as both are for their own good. (7.1.25)

2. The Fallacy of Material Life

Material life is called '*pavarga*' because here we are subject to five different states of suffering, represented by the letters *pa, pha, ba, bha* and *ma*. *Pa* means *pariśrama* or hard labor. *Pha* means *phena* or foam from mouth due to labor. *Ba* means *byarthatā*, disappointment despite hard labor. *Bha* means *bhaya* or fear due to not knowing what will happen next. *Ma* means *mṛtyu* or death. By practicing *kṛṣṇa-bhakti,* one can give up this '*pvarga*' and attain '*apavarga*' or liberation.

The following compilation lists various verses on the fallacy of materialistic life as described in the chapters of Canto Seven. For more details the readers may refer to the respective verses and chapters.

Root of materalism

- **Forgetfulness leads to misery:** The conditioned soul forgets his self-interest (his eternal relationship with Kṛṣṇa) due to bodily identification. Attracted by the varieties of the material world, he suffers. (7.13.28)
- **The Lord's māyā** has created the material conception of life that distinguishes people as 'friends' and 'enemies.' (7.5.11)

Not a good option

- **Blind well:** The soul-degrading materialistic household life is like a blind well, full of anxieties, with minds absorbed in "I and mine" conception. One should come out of it by taking shelter of Lord Hari. (7.5.5 *tat sādhu manye 'sura-varya...*)
- **Calculated analysis:** The 100 years of human life are wasted by 50 years in sleep, 20 years in childhood, 20 years in oldage and the remaining years in family attachments. (7.6.6-8)
- **Strength of material attachment:** Who can give up desire for money (*artha-tṛṣṇāṁ*), which is dearer than one's life? Thieves, servants and merchants try to get money even by risking their lives. (7.6.10)
- **Insubstantial:** The happiness and blessings in this world are as insubstantial as a mirage in a desert. (7.9.25 *kutrāśiṣaḥ śruti-sukhā mṛgatṛṣṇi-rūpāḥ...*)

- **Ignorance:** Even the learned are overcome by ignorance absorbed in family affairs, incapable of understanding oneself. (7.6.16)
- **Insignificant:** The material happiness of household life and sex life is insignificant. (7.9.45 *yan maithunādi-gṛhamedhi-sukhaṁ hi tucchaṁ…*)
- **Cause of concern:** Great devotees like Prahlāda are very much concerned about the suffering conditioned souls. (7.9.43-44 *naivodvije para duratyaya…*)
- **Materialists are** ignorant, ambitious, misled and entangled (7.5.31 *na te viduḥ svārtha-gatiṁ hi viṣṇuṁ…*)

Based on a faulty assumption

- **Troublesome remedies:** The remedies to material dualities and more miserable than the miseries themselves. (7.9.17 *yasmāt priyāpriya-viyoga-saṁyoga-janma…*)
- **Illusory happiness:** A man and a woman unite for sex pleasure, but they actually do not become happy. Material sense enjoyment is simply an imagination. Spiritual happiness is real happiness, and it can be achieved only when one stops all materialistic activities. (7.13.26-27)
- **Insatiable:** Family attachments – with wife, children, parents, daughter, furniture and so on – are insatiable (7.6.11-13)
- **Analogy:** Just as a deer cannot see the water within a covered well, but runs after a mirage, the conditioned soul does not see happiness within oneself, but runs for it elsewhere. But all of one's plans are ultimately baffled. (7.13.29-31)
- **Example:** In spite of controlling all directions and enjoying all kinds of sense gratification, Hiraṇyakaśipu was dissatisfied due to uncontrolled senses. (7.4.19)

Consequences

- The attached householders' inclination towards Kṛṣṇa is never aroused by (*i*) others' instructions (*ii*) own efforts or (*iii*) a combination of both. Due to uncontrolled senses, they enter hellish life and repeatedly chew the chewed. (7.5.30 *matir na kṛṣṇe parataḥ svato vā…*)
- **Frustration:** A materialist (*karmī*) is frustrated in his attempts to attain better enjoyment. (7.7.41-42)
- **No space for the Lord:** The sinful material mind absorbed in lusty desires cannot think of the Supreme Lord's activities (7.9.39 *naitan manas tava kathāsu…*)
- **Transmigration** caused due to insatiable material desires. (7.13.24)
- **Binding:** An attached householder with uncontrolled senses, is bound strongly by ropes of affection for his family and cannot be liberated. (7.6.9)

- **Embarrassment:** The ever-distracted senses constantly embarrass the conditioned soul who is like a person with many wives. (7.9.40 *jihvaikato 'cyuta vikarṣati...*)

Ultimately ends in failure

- **Temporary:** The happiness offered by ephemeral riches, wife, animals, children, residence and other luxuries is perishable in a moment. (7.7.39 *rāyaḥ kalatraṁ paśavaḥ sutādayo...*) Even heavenly happiness is temporary. (7.7.40)
- **Perishable:** The material body, its possessions and relations are all perishable and sources of misery (7.7.43-47)
- **Constant fear:** Even a wealthy man is insecure due to being a victim of senses, and out of fear of government laws, thieves, enemies, family members, animals, beggars and so on. (7.13.32-33)
- **Defeat:** Absorption in family maintenance (*kuṭumba-poṣa*) leads to exhaustion of lifespan and defeat of the real purpose of human life. (7.6.14-15)
- One's long life, opulence and power will be vanquished within a moment. (7.9.23)

Solution: How to let go of materialism

- **When Lord is pleased** – (*i*) one's animal intelligence (*paśu-buddhi*) is destroyed and (*ii*) one doesn't make distinctions of friends and enemies. (7.5.12)
- By Serving Lotus Feet of Devotees: one can come out of materialistic life (7.5.32 *naiṣāṁ matis tāvad urukramāṅghriṁ...*)
- **Performing bhakti:** Material happiness of the senses can be obtained automatically. One need not endeavour for it separately. It is better to utilize one's human life to perform *bhakti*. (7.6.3-5)
- **Solution:** By keeping aloof from the association of demons and taking shelter of Lord Nārāyaṇa, one can be liberated from material bondage. (7.6.18)
- **Destroying the material intelligence** by Kṛṣṇa consciousness: Polluted intelligence entangles the *jīva* in material life and three modes. (7.7.27-28)
- **By knowing the negative effects** of material desires, a devotee desires not to have any material desires. (7.10.7-9)
- **An intelligent person should give up** desire for prestige and money, which is the cause of lamentation, illusion, fear, anger, attachment, poverty, unnecessary labor etc. (7.13.34 *śoka-moha-bhaya-krodha...*)
- **By hearing about Kṛṣṇa** in good Association, one gradually becomes detached from family affection, exactly like a man awakening from a dream. (7.14.4)
- **Cultivating satisfaction** by giving up greed for material things. (7.15.15-21)

3. The Glories of a Guru

A bona fide *guru* is one who guides us towards the shelter of God. Seeking the guidance of a *guru* constitutes the most vital aspect of one's spiritual life. Prahlāda Mahārāja had two kinds of *gurus*—Śaṇḍa and Amarka who taught him materialistic subjects, and Nārada Muni who who instructed him in transcendental science. Thus Nārada Muni is Prahlāda's real *guru*. The following compilation presents the importance of a *guru* as described in various chapters of the Seventh Canto.

Qualification of a Guru

- **Definition:** The word *guru* refers to the spiritual master who initiates his disciple into advancement in the science of Kṛṣṇa, or Kṛṣṇa consciousness. (7.4.31-32)
- **Paramparā:** An actual *guru* is *śrotriya*, one who has heard or received perfect knowledge through *paramparā*, the disciplic succession. (7.5.31)
- **Order of Lord Śrī Caitanya:** One must become a sincere servant of Kṛṣṇa. One should become a guru and spread Kṛṣṇa consciousness all over the world. (CC Madhya 7.128 *yāre dekha, tāre kaha 'kṛṣṇa'-upadeśa…*) (7.9.41)

Guru is as good as God, but not God

- In all the scriptures, spiritual master is considered to be as good as Lord. This does not mean, however, that Vaiṣṇava thinks himself God, but remains a faithful servant of the Lord and never tries to enjoy the prestige that might accrue to him from being the Supreme Lord's representative. (7.14.40-42 P)

Purpose of a Guru

- **Gives Shelter:** When one is perplexed by the problems of life, one must approach a *guru* like Nārada or his representative in the disciplic succession. [MU 1.2.12 *tad-vijñānārthaṁ sa gurum evābhigacchet…*] (7.1.21)
- **Guide:** Human form is a most valuable boat, the spiritual master is the captain, *guru-karṇadhāram*, to guide the boat, and the instructions of Kṛṣṇa are favorable breeze. One must use all these facilities to cross the ocean of nescience. (7.15.45)
- **A representative of Kṛṣṇa** only gives perfect knowledge to his disciple. (7.15.76)

- **Kṛṣṇa as guru:** Kṛṣṇa helps as the *guru*, from within and from without. From without He helps the devotee as His representative, and from within He talks personally with the pure devotee and gives him instructions. (7.15.76)

First guru-seva, then Kṛṣṇa-seva

- **Guru before Kṛṣṇa:** Kṛṣṇa does not become the direct spiritual master unless one is fully trained by His representative spiritual master. (7.15.76)
- **Vaiṣṇava Principle:** One should not bypass the spiritual master and desire to serve the Supreme Lord. One should serve the spiritual master first. (7.9.28)

Service to Guru

- **Cross ocean of nescience:** By satisfying Guru, one automatically pleases Kṛṣṇa and gets the strength to cross the ocean of nescience. (7.15.28, 45)
- **God realization:** By staunch faith in the spiritual master and the Supreme Lord, one not only controls the senses but also realizes the Supreme Lord. (7.15.28)
- **Imports of Vedic knowledge are revealed** to those who have implicit faith in both the Lord and the spiritual master (ŚU 6.23 *yasya deve parā bhaktir…*)
- **Aspiration of devotees:** To be in touch with pure devotee and serve him as a sincere servant. (7.9.24 *kālātmanopanaya māṁ nija-bhṛtya-pārśvam…*)
- **First priority:** Devotees feel their first duty is to serve *guru*, for he instructs to one achieve transcendental position. (7.9.28 *so 'haṁ kathaṁ nu visṛje…*)
- **Beginning of spiritual life:** *Guru-pādāśrayaḥ*. By following the instructions of the *guru* and the *śāstras*, a disciple attains the stage of devotional service and becomes unattached to material possessions. (7.7.33)
- **Brahmacārī:** With a great vow, a *brahmacārī* lives at the *guru-kula*, only for the benefit of the *guru*. He should be submissive and friendly to the *guru*. (7.12.1)
- **Perfection:** Only one who executes spiritual life under the direction of spiritual master can achieve mercy of Kṛṣṇa. *yasya prasādād bhagavat-prasādaḥ*. (7.12.11)

Material Guru

- **Other Interests:** Prahlāda Mahārāja did not recognize seminal spiritual master, who are not at all interested in Viṣṇu. Indeed, they are hopeful of material success (*bahir-artha-māninaḥ*). (7.5.31)
- **Blind:** Gurus, teachers, who are simply interested in this material world are described as *andha*, blind. (7.5.31)

4. Prayers: A Supplication for Grace

In difficulty, doubt or overwhelming love, faithful devotees express themselves to the Supreme Lord in prayer and glorification. They don't seek any material remuneration, nor benefits from the Lord – but simply seek His shelter, remembrance and love. The following table gives a bird's eyeview of the prayers offered by various devotees in Canto Seven.

	Personality	Situation	Purpose	Theme	Result
1	The demigods (7.4.22-23)	Disturbed due to the punishment inflicted by powerful Hiraṇyakaśipu.	In distress obliged to seek shelter of the Lord.	Obeisances to Lord Hṛṣīkeśa and to the direction where He resides.	The Lord told them to wait patiently, till He counteracts Hiraṇyakaśipu
2	Demigods, sages and other (7.8.40-56)	After killing Hiraṇyakaśipu Lord Nṛsiṁha angrily sat on his throne	To pacify the Lord	Thanking Lord for saving them by killing demon Hiraṇyakaśipu	Lord was still angry
3	Prahlāda Mahārāja (7.9.8-50)	Demigods, Lord Brahmā, Śiva and even Lakṣmījī dared not to approach Lord	To appease the Lord	Devotion and surrender unto the Lord, gratitude for devotees	Lord Nṛsiṁha-deva was pacified
4	Prahlāda Mahārāja (7.10.2-10)	Lord allures him by offering him benedictions	Desiring only pure devotional service	"I am Your unmotivated servant. Make me free of all material desires"	The Lord offers Prahlāda benedictions
5	Prahlāda Mahārāja (7.10.15-17)	Lord Nṛsiṁha offers benediction	Requesting the Lord to excuse Hiraṇyakaśipu from sinful reactions		Entire dynasty already purified

5. The Dynamics of Lust

For a spiritual seeker, lust or desire for material enjoyment, specifically sex pleasure, is a great enemy. Several sections of *Śrīmad-Bhāgavatam* describe the dangers of lust along with fitting examples of personalities who became victims of lust. The following are some references from the Seventh Canto on this topic.

Degrees of Lust

- **Seed of material existence:** Prahlāda states that the root cause of material exsisence is the seed of lusty desires in the core of everyone's heart (7.10.3)
- **Spiritual lust:** Six *anarthas kāma, krodha, lobha, moha, mada* and *mātsarya* all have their proper use for the Supreme Lord and His devotee. (7.9.1 P)
- Even great devotees think that they are under the influence of lust: Prahlāda says "My dear Lord my mind is extremely sinful and lusty" (7.9.39)

Regulation of Lust

- **Concession:** Among four ashrams, only *gṛhastha* is given permission by the *guru* to indulge in sex during the period favourable for procreation. (7.12.12 P)
- **Determination:** By making plans with determination, one should give up lusty desires for sense gratification. (7.15.22)

Liberation from lust

- **Absorption:** This great attention towards the Lord even may be due to lusty desires (*parakiya* and *svakīya*). The *gopīs* by their lusty desires obtained the mercy of Kṛṣṇa. (7.1.30-31)
- **Servitude:** By service to *guru*, hearing, glorification and remembrance of the Lord, deity worship, saintly association, offering due respect to all living entities, one can cut down the influence lust and attain loving service to the Lord. (7.7.32-33)
- **Yoga:** Prahlāda always controlled his senses and life air, and being of steady intelligence and determination, he subdued all lusty desires. (7.4.33)

Effect of Lust

- **Unhappiness:** One who is content and satisfied serving the Supreme Lord, enjoys happiness without endeavouring for his livelihood. Where is such happiness for a materialistic man who being impelled by lust and greed, wanders in all directions with a desire to accumulate wealth? (7.15.16)
- **Anger:** Lust, anger and greed are the causes of the conditioned soul's bondage in this material world. (Bg. 3.37 *kāma eṣa krodha eṣa...*) And when strong lusty desires are unfulfilled, one becomes angry. (7.15.20)
- **Contrary Results:** In this human life, men and women unite for the sensual pleasure of sex, but it is observed that none of them are happy. Therefore, seeing the contrary results, I have stopped taking part in materialistic activities. (7.13.26)
- **Disturbed:** When one's consciousness is uncontaminated by material lusty desires, it becomes calm and peaceful in all activities, for one is situated in eternal blissful life. (7.15.35)
- **Losses from Lust:** Because of lusty desires from the very beginning of one's birth, the functions of one's senses, mind, life, body, religion, patience, intelligence, shyness, opulence, strength, memory and truthfulness are vanquished. (7.10.8)
- **Lust leads to ignorance:** When one is too attached to material enjoyment, he is bereft of all knowledge. (BG 7.20 *kāmais tais tair hṛta-jñānāḥ...*) (7.10.2 P)

Analogies of Lust

- **Lusty absorption:** Just as absorption of lusty man in women is deep one should be fully absorbed in thoughts of Kṛṣṇa (7.1.27)
- **Overindulgence:** Just as drops of ghee on a fire never extinguish the fire but a flood of ghee will, overindulgence in lusty desires mitigates such desires entirely. Low born and sinful people are allowed to enjoy sinful acts fully, for thus there is a chance that these activities will become detestful to them, and they will get the opportunity to be purified. (7.11.33-34)
- **Itching:** Sex life is compared to the rubbing of two hands to relieve an itch. Gṛhamedhis, who have no spiritual knowledge, think that this itching is the greatest platform of happiness, although actually it is a source of distress. The *kṛpaṇas*, the fools are not satisfied by repeated sensuous enjoyment. Those who are *dhīra*, the sober tolerate this itching, are not subjected to the sufferings of fools and rascals. (7.9.45)

APPENDIX

1. Character Portrayals

Śrīmad-Bhāgavatam is a string of episodes describing the qualities and activities of the Supreme Lord, His various incarnations and His devotees. Just as hearing about the Lord is repeatedly emphasized in the *Bhāgavatam*, hearing about the devotees is also given similar importance. Pure devotees give us inspiration through their example, enlightenment through their teachings and direction through their instructions.

The qualities of great devotees like Prahlāda Mahārāja are very enlivening to meditating upon. Similarly, negative charatcers of demons like Hiraṇyakaśipu give is a caution note on the unfavourable attitudes. The following is a short compilation on the characters of Prahlāda and Hiraṇyakaśipu to help us understand what is favourable and unfavourable for our spiritual practice.

Prahlāda Mahārāja

Life

- **Lineage**: Son of *asura* king *Hiraṇyakaśipu* and his mother was *Kayādhu.* He had three well-qualified brothers. (7.4.30)
- **Education:** He got spiritual education in the womb of his mother from Nārada Muni, but he was taught material topics in the school of Śaṇḍa and Amarka. (7.5.2)
- **Prolong rule:** He ruled *asuras* until the end of the duration of time occupied by *Manu*. (7.10.11)

Divine Qualities

- **Mahājana:** Prahlāda Mahārāja was one of the twelve Mahājanas.
- **Mahā-bhāgavata:** Just as everything appears yellow to the jaundiced eye, similarly, to Prahlāda, a *mahā-bhāgavata*, everyone but himself appeared to be engaged in Kṛṣṇa's service. (7.4.37P)
- **No enemies:** He was *nirvairāya* (7.4.28). He did not like political philosophy involves considering someone a friend and someone else an enemy. (7.5.3).

- **Brāhmaṇa:** Prahlāda was an *asura* by birth, yet he possessed all the qualities of a perfect *brāhmaṇa* (*brahmaṇyaḥ śīla-sampannaḥ*), having very good character and determinination to understand the Absolute Truth. (7.4.32-33 P)
- **Delivered clan:** Prahlāda asked the Lord to deliver his father and the Lord delivered twenty one generations of forefathers. (7.10.18)
- **Best friend:** Like the Supersoul, he was kind to every living entity and was the best friend of everyone. (7.4.31)
- **Fitting dealings:** To respectable persons he acted exactly like a menial servant, to the poor he was like a father, to his equals he was attached like a sympathetic brother. (7.4.32)
- **Respectful:** He considered his teachers, spiritual masters and older Godbrothers to be as good as the Supreme Personality of Godhead. (7.4.32)
- **Faith in guru:** He simply followed the instructions of Nārada Muni, his *guru*, and thus he always remained a stalwart devotee. (7.13.45 P)
- **Obedient:** He accepted words of Brahmā to pacify lord. (7.9.4)
- **Modest:** He was completely free from unnatural pride that might have arisen from his good education, riches, beauty, aristocracy and so on. (7.4.32)
- **Detached:** Even as a small boy, he had no interest in playing or other material activities. (7.4.37)

- **Materially callous:** Prahlāda didn't give any importance to anything in this world, knowing that even the powerful, opulent or influential, can not endure. (7.9.23 P)
- **Realized soul:** He had no interests in his father's property. He thought whether one is in the heaven or hell or is a rich or a poor man's son, material conditions are everywhere. Therefore no condition of life is at all pleasing. (7.9.17 P)
- **Grateful:** As a Vaiṣṇava, despite all the inconveniences imposed upon him by his father, he could not forget his father's affection. (7.10.15-17 P)
- **Felt unqualified:** He said to the Lord that he was low class yet the Lord had placed His lotus hands upon his head. (7.9.26)
- **Sense controlled:** He always controlled his senses and life air, and being of steady intelligence and determination, he subdued all lusty desires. (7.4.33)
- **Undisturbed:** He was not agitated when put into danger, and he was neither directly nor indirectly interested in the Vedic fruitive activities and was completely devoid of material desires. (7.4.33)
- **Fearless:** He fearlessly advised Hiraṇyakaśipu to surrender to Viṣṇu (7.5.24). He approached to pacify the fearsome Lord Nṛsiṁha-deva whom even goddess Lakṣmī could not approach. (7.9.4)
- **Confident:** He was confident that Kṛṣṇa would give him full protection under all circumstances. (7.8.7 P)
- **Humble:** Although Prahlāda Mahārāja was a pure, exalted Vaiṣṇava, he thought himself most unqualified to offer prayers to the Supreme Lord. (7.9.8 P)
- **Doesn't waste time:** At the opportune moment when it was possible to preach about Kṛṣṇa consciousness, he taught his classmates. He wanted to utilize every moment for advancing in Kṛṣṇa consciousness. (7.5.54 P)
- **Cognizant:** Prahlāda knew the best of knowledge, and when his father inquired from him, he gave him that knowledge. Prahlāda was able to solve the most difficult parts of problems because of his advanced Kṛṣṇa consciousness (7.5.4 P)
- **Kṛṣṇa conscious vision:** Just as those who are greedy see everything as a source of money-making and those who are lusty see everything as being conducive to sex, Prahlāda saw Nārāyaṇa even within a stone column (*sthāvara-jaṅgama dekhe...*). (7.4.37 P)
- **Eager to attain Lord:** Prahlāda Mahārāja expected that the Lord, by His kindness, would call him again to the shelter of His lotus feet. (7.9.16 P)
- **Special quality:** Prahlāda still lives in Vaikuṇṭhaloka as well as within this material world on the planet Sutala, just like the Supreme Lord. (7.4.34 P)
- **Compassionate:** He does not want be benefited alone, rather, he prays to the Lord that all of us fallen souls in this material world may be delivered. (7.9.42 P)

- **Devine aspiration:** Did not want to enjoy the estate left by his father; rather, he wanted to become a servant of the servant of the Lord and remain in touch with pure devotee. (7.9.24 P)

Complete absorption in Kṛṣṇa

- **Kṛṣṇa-graha-gṛhītātmā**
  - Since his mind was always affected by Kṛṣṇa consciousness, he couldn't understand how the world goes on absorbed in sense gratification. (7.4.37)
  - He sometimes cried, sometimes laughed, sometimes expressed jubilation and sometimes sang loudly. (7.4.39)
- **Govinda-parirambhitaḥ**
  - Prahlāda being always embraced by the Lord, he did not know how his bodily necessities, such as sitting, walking, eating, lying down, drinking and talking, were being automatically performed. (7.4.38)
  - He was always protected by the Supreme Lord just as a child on the lap of his father or mother. (7.5.41 P)
  - He had Full faith in the Lord's protection (7.9.22 P)
  - Nārada Muni told demigods that they will not be able to kill child Prahlāda even in the womb. (7.7.10)

HIRAṆYAKAŚIPU

- **Family:** Hiraṇyakaśipu had four wonderful, well-qualified sons, of whom the one named Prahlāda was the best. His wife was Kayādhu. (7.4.30)
- **Interest:** Hiraṇyakaśipu was simply interested in gold and sense enjoyment. The word *hiraṇya* means "gold," and *kaśipu* refers to soft cushions and bedding on which people enjoy sense gratification. (7.5.18)
- **Different births:** The associates of Lord Viṣṇu, Jaya and Vijaya, had descended to the material world to serve the Lord by fulfilling His desire to fight. Their three different births were: first as Hiraṇyākṣa and Hiraṇyakaśipu, second as Rāvaṇa and Kumbhakarṇa, and third as Śiśupāla and Dantavakra (7.1.35 P)
- **Inimical to Viṣṇu**
  - Hiraṇyakaśipu accused the Lord of being partial to demigods because the demigods worshiped Him. (7.2.6 P)
  - Hiraṇyakaśipu thought that the Lord can change His mind at any time and therefore His words and activities are like those of children. (7.2.7-8P)
  - He wanted to offer blood of Viṣṇu to please his brother Hiraṇyākṣa. (7.2.7-8)

- **Demoniac plans**
  - Hiraṇyakaśipu planned to kill the inhabitants of earth so that *yajña* would stop and the demigods, being disturbed, would die automatically when Lord Viṣṇu, the *yajñeśvara*, was killed. (7.2.10 P)
  - Hiraṇyakaśipu planned to destroy the brahminical culture and the *kṣatriya* government and thus create chaos all over the world. (7.2.11 P)
- **Knowledgeable but demonic intelligence**
  - He was a great politician and so he knew how to act according to the time and situation (7.2.18-19)
  - He had Vedic knowledge and understanding. He gave sound advice to his family members on his brother's death, to pacify them. But he did not used his good intelligence for the service of the Lord. 7.2.21P
  - He carefully asked Brahmā for benedictions that will be almost as good as immortality. (7.3.35P)
- **Asuric determination**
  - Hiraṇyakaśipu wanted to usurp the position of Lord Brahmā (7.3.10)
  - He wanted to reverse the results of pious and impious acts. He wanted those promoted to the heavenly planets, to become unhappy and suffer. (7.3.11 P)
  - He wanted to destroy brahminical culture and protection of cows. (7.3.13)
- **Severe austerity**
  - Hiraṇyakaśipu's body was covered by an anthill and by grass and bamboo sticks. (7.13.15-16)
  - The ants had devoured his skin, fat, flesh and blood. (7.13.15-16)

  - Even Brahmā was struck with wonder to see Hiraṇyakaśipu's extraordinary power to execute *tapasya*. (7.13.15-16 P)
- **Demoniac Power**
  - Hiraṇyakaśipu conquered all the planets in the three worlds (7.4.5-7)
  - All the demigods except Lord Brahmā, Lord Śiva and Lord Viṣṇu were forced to engage in his service. (7.4.9-10)
  - Instead of offering shares of the oblations in a sacrifice to the demigods, he accepted them himself. (7.4.15)
  - He always transgressed the laws and regulations mentioned in the authoritative *śāstras*.
- **Dissatisfied:** Although so powerful and controller of all directions, was dissatisfied because instead of controlling his senses he remained their servant. (7.4.19 P)
- **Relationship with Prahlāda**
- **Plans for Prahlāda**
  - He wanted Prahlāda Mahārāja to be trained as a diplomatic king in ruling the kingdom. (7.5.51P)
  - Hiraṇyakaśipu wanted to keep Prahlāda in mundane attachment. (7.5.51 P)
- **Affectionate attitude towards son changed**
  - When he saw that his son has become devotee of Viṣṇu, he threw him off his lap and onto the ground and ordered him to be killed. (7.5.33-34)
  - He was perplexed about how his five-year-old boy could be so fearless that he did not care for the order of his very great and powerful father. (7.8.6 P)
- **Delivered by son:** Although Hiraṇyakaśipu was extremely inimical toward the Supreme Personality of Godhead, he always thought of his son, Prahlāda, who was a great devotee. By the grace of his son, he was delivered by the Lord. (7.1.26 P)

2. Kṛṣṇa's Names

The Supreme Personality of Godhead, Lord Kṛṣṇa is unlimited and so are His names. Unlike an ordinary human, the Lord's names indicate His various forms, qualities and activities. It is amazing to note how many different ways Śukadeva Gosvāmī, Nārada Muni and others in the *Śrīmad-Bhāgavatam* addressed and described the Supreme Lord. These names reflect His personal attributes and divine character. The following is a list of prominent names of Lord Kṛṣṇa and His special form as Nṛsiṁha-deva, as described the Seventh Canto. Although some of these names appear repeatedly, only one instance of the name is given below.

	Ref	Name	Meaning
1	7.8.44	*akhila-dharma-goptra*	The Lord who maintains universal religious principles
2	7.9.40	*acyuta*	The infallible Lord
3	7.10.10	*adbhuta-siṁha*	Nṛsiṁha-deva wjo has a wonderful lionlike form
4	7.7.37	*adhokṣaja*	One who is beyond the reach of the materialistic mind or experimental knowledge
5	7.6.18	*ādi-deva*	The origin of all demigods
6	7.8.43	*ādi-puruṣa*	The original Personality of Godhead
7	7.1.6	*ajaḥ*	The unborn Lord
8	7.9.15	*ajita*	Supreme victorious person, never conquered by anyone
9	7.10.26	*akhila-adhyakṣa*	Owner of the whole universe
10	7.1.25	*akhila-ātmana*	Supersoul of all living entities
11	7.9.42	*akhila-guu*	Supreme spiritual master of the entire creation
12	7.8.34	*alakṣita-dvairatham*	One whose challenger or enemy was not seen
13	7.9.29	*ananta*	Reservoir of unlimited divine qualities
14	7.6.22	*anirdeśyaḥ*	One who cannot be described
15	7.6.22	*anubhava-*	One whose form is blissful and full of knowledge

		ānanda-svarūpaḥ	
16	7.9.10	*aravinda-nābha*	Viṣṇu, who has a lotus growing from His navel
17	7.9.50	*arhat-tama*	Supreme of all worshipable persons
18	7.9.42	*ārta-bandu*	Friend of the suffering living entities
19	7.9.47	*arūpaka*	The Lord, who possess no material form
20	7.6.2	*ātma-īśvaraḥ*	The master of the soul, the Supersoul
21	7.8.41	*bhakta-vatsala*	Lord, who are so affectionate to His devotee
22	7.10.26	*bhūta-bhāvana*	Cause of all living entities
23	7.10.42	*brahmaṇya-deva*	The Lord who is worshiped by all brāhmaṇas
24	7.5.14	*cakra-pāṇi*	Lord Viṣṇu, who has a disc in His hand
25	7.8.56	*śaraṇa-da*	The everlasting bestower of shelter
26	7.8.43	*śaraṇya-pāla*	Supreme maintainer of those who need shelter
27	7.1.25	*dama-kartuḥ*	The supreme controller
28	7.11.5	*dharma-setu*	The Lord who protects religious principles
29	7.4.38	*govinda*	The Lord who enlivens the senses
30	7.8.8	*guṇa-traya-īśaḥ*	The master of the material modes
31	7.4.23	*hṛṣīkeśa*	The master of the senses
32	7.8.56	*hari-nara*	Half lion and half human being
33	7.7.49	*hari*	The Lord who mitigates miseries of all *jīvas*
34	7.7.37	*hṛt-īśvara*	The Supersoul within the heart.
35	7.14.42	*jagat-ātmana*	One who is the life and soul of the whole creation
36	7.8.12	*jagat-īśvara*	The supreme controller of the universe
37	7.9.24	*kāla-ātmanā*	The master of the time factor
38	7.9.16	*kṛpaṇa-vatsala*	The Lord, who is very kind to the fallen souls (who have no spiritual knowledge)
39	7.10.4	*karuṇā-ātmana*	The Lord who is extremely kind to His devotees
40	7.1.38	*madhu-dviṣaḥ*	Viṣṇu, the slayer of the Madhu demon
41	7.10.10	*mahā-ātma*	The Supreme Soul, or the Supersoul
42	7.8.53	*mahā-puruṣa*	The Supreme Personality of Godhead
43	7.7.50	*mukunda*	Lord Kṛṣṇa, who can give liberation
44	7.8.39	*nara-śārdulam*	Lord, who had appeared as half man and half lion
45	7.10.25	*nara-harim*	Lord Nṛsiṁha-deva
46	7.6.27	*nara-sakhaḥ*	The friend of all living entities (especially humans)
47	7.9.11	*nija-lābha-pūrṇaḥ*	One who is always satisfied in Himself (does not depend on others' service)
48	7.1.6	*nirguṇaḥ*	One who is without material qualities
49	7.8.49	*para-īśa*	The Supreme Lord

50	7.9.18	*paradevatā*	The Supreme Personality of Godhead
51	7.10.48	*param brahma*	The Supreme Personality of Godhead
52	7.6.22	*parama-īśvaraḥ*	The supreme ruler
53	7.8.40	*pavitra-karmaṇe*	The Lord whose actions have no reaction
54	7.1.6	*prakṛteḥ-paraḥ*	Transcendental to material nature
55	7.10.9	*puṇḍarīka-akṣa*	The lotus-eyed Lord
56	7.10.26	*pūrva-ja*	The original Personality of Godhead
57	7.1.43	*sama-darśana*	The Lord who is equal to everyone
58	7.11.12	*sarva-ātmā*	The Supreme Lord, the Supersoul of all
59	7.7.53	*sarva-bhūta-ātmani*	One who is situated as the soul and Supersoul of all living entities
60	7.14.17	*sarva-yajña-bhuk*	The enjoyer of the results of all kinds of sacrifices
61	7.8.24	*sattva-dhāmani*	The Lord who is situated in pure goodness
62	7.8.49	*sattva-mūrti*	Transcendental form of pure goodness
63	7.1.41	*siṁha-rūpi*	The form of a lion (Lord Narasiṁha)
64	7.6.2	*suhṛt*	The best well-wisher and friend
65	7.12.2	*surottama*	Lord Viṣṇu, Puruṣottama, the best of personalities
66	7.1.12	*uru-śrava*	The Lord whose glories are widespread
67	7.8.23	*uru-māyi*	One who possesses the great mystic power
68	7.9.49	*urugāya*	Supreme Lord, who is glorified by all saintly men
69	7.8.8	*urukrama*	The Lord, whose every action is uncommon;
70	7.4.42	*uttama-śloka*	The Lord who is worshiped by divine prayers
71	7.10.7	*varada-ṛṣabha*	The Supreme Lord, who can give any benediction;
72	7.8.34	*vibhu*	The Supreme Lord
73	7.8.40	*vicitra-vīrya*	The Lord who has varieties of prowess
74	7.9.39	*vikuṇṭha-nātha*	Lord of Vaikuṇṭha, where there is no anxiety

3. Analogies

Conveying a message becomes simple and easy when explained through an analogy. We find analogies used commonly in our scriptures and even day-to-day life. Several speakers in the *Bhāgavatam* like Śukadeva Gosvāmī and Nārada Muni used fitting analogies to present deep philosophical points and Śrīla Prabhupāda further elaborates on these messages with contemporary analogies the modern man can relate to. The following is a list of analogies from the verses and purports of the Seventh Canto of *Śrīmad Bhāgavatam*.

> **Note:** Subjects/ objects/ things marked with same color are compared with each other within a particular analogy. Example: **Fire** – **Lord**, **friction** – **krpa-śakti.**

About the Supreme Lord

1. The **sun** drives away the **darkness of the universe**, similarly the **Lord** always drives away all the **darkness of ignorance**. (7.13.22)
2. Just as **real law** is that which is given by the **government**, the **real religion** is that which is given by the **Supreme Lord**. (7.15.13 P)
3. Just as a **desire tree** delivers **fruits** according to **one's desires**, **the Lord** offer **benedictions** according to the **level of one's service**. (7.9.27 P)
4. An **electrician** connects both **a heater** and **a cooler** to the **same electrical energy**. The cause of the heating and cooling is **his manipulation of the electrical energy**. The **Supreme Lord** is **equal to everyone**. When **the demigods** are favored and **the demons** are killed, this is not His partiality but the **influence of time.** (7.1.12 P)
5. A **criminal is put in prison** and punished by the **government**, but the same government, if it likes, can release him. Similarly, **our material condition of suffering** has been allotted to us by the **Supreme Lord**, and if we want to be saved from this suffering, we must appeal to Him. (7.9.22 P)
6. One can understand the supply of **fire** in **wood**, the **water** in a **waterpot**, or the **sky** within a **pot**. Similarly an expert thinker can perceive how the **Supreme Lord** is present within the **heart** of every living being. (7.1.9)

7. When **cotton** is transformed into **thread**, the cotton is no longer visible, and when the **thread** is woven into **cloth**, the thread is no longer visible. Similarly, the **seed** that had generated from the navel of Garbhodakaśāyī Viṣṇu became manifested as the **cosmic creation**, one could no longer understand where the cause of the cosmos is. (7.9.34 P)
8. **Worms** captured by a **black drone** obtain the **same type of body** as the drone. Similarly, **demons** killed by the **Supreme Lord** receive spiritual bodies and forms same as the Lord, because of thinking about the Him at death. (7.10.39)

About the Living Entities

9. The **moon** and the **sun** are extremely **brilliant** and can be directly perceived, but when covered by **clouds**, they are not distinctly visible. Similarly, the more **one** advances in goodness, the more his **brilliance** is exhibited by *bhakti*, but the more one is covered by **passion** and **ignorance**, the less visible his brilliance. (7.1.9 P)
10. A **grassworm** confined in a hole by a **bee** always thinks of the bee in fear and enmity and later becomes a bee. Similarly, if the **conditioned souls** somehow or other think of **Kṛṣṇa** as their worshipable Lord or even an enemy, by such constant thinking they will regain their spiritual bodies. (7.1.28-29)
11. Just as **many travelers** come together in a **restaurant**, and later continue to their respective destinations, the **living entities** join together in a **family**, and later, as a result of their own actions, they are led apart to their destinations. (7.2.21)
12. **Criminal prisoners** scatter as soon as their terms are over and they are released. Similarly, **all of us** who have temporarily assembled as family members will continue to our respective destinations. (7.2.21)
13. A **householder**, although different from the identity of his **house**, thinks his house to be identical with him. Similarly, the **conditioned soul**, due to ignorance, accepts the **body** to be himself, although the body is actually different from the soul. (7.2.42 P)
14. Just as **fire** in **wood** is different from the wood, as **air** within the **mouth** and **nostrils** is separate, and as the all-pervading **sky** never mixes with **anything**, similarly, the **living entity**, although now encaged within the **material body**, is separate from it. (7.2.43 P)
15. Just as every **part of the body** is meant to serve the **whole body**, similarly every **living entity**, being part of the **Supreme Lord**, is meant to serve the Lord. (7.5.11 P)
16. Just as there is no difficulty in establishing intimate relationship between a **father** and **son**, there is no difficulty in re-establishing the natural, intimate relationship between **Supreme Lord** and the **living entities**. (7.6.19 P)
17. Just as a **drop** of seawater is composed of the same chemicals as the great **sea** itself, the **living entities** have the same qualities as the **Lord**. (7.7.20 P)

18. One can understand the presence of the **air** by the **aromas** it carries. Similarly, one can understand the **living soul** by three **divisions of intelligence** i.e. wakefulness, dreaming and deep sleep under the guidance of Supreme Lord. (7.7.26)
19. Just as there are **different grades of fire**, but all of them derive heat and light from the **sun, all living entities**, big or small, are dependent on the mercy of the **Supreme Lord**. (7.8.7 P)
20. Just as **small piece of grass falls** in a **river** and is tossed about with different types of wood and tree branches, similarly, the **living entity floats** in the **ocean of material existence** and is dashed and tossed amidst material conditions. (7.13.24)
21. Just as a **deer** cannot see the **water** within a well covered by **grass**, but runs after water elsewhere, the **living entity** covered by the **material body** does not see the **happiness** within himself, but runs after happiness in the material world. (7.13.29)
22. Just as a **wheel** sometimes **goes up** and sometimes **comes down**, similarly the stringent laws of material nature makes the **living entity** in material existence sometimes **happy** and sometimes **distressed.** (7.13.30 P)

Material Conditioning

23. Just as both **gold** and **iron** are metal, but there is a vast difference in their value, so, there is difference in **lusty desires of the gopīs** and **material lusty desires.** (7.1.31 P)
24. **Fruits** and **flowers** of a tree in due course of time undergo six changes—birth, existence, growth, transformation, dwindling and then death. Similarly the **material body**, which is obtained by the spirit soul, undergoes similar changes. (7.7.18 P)
25. A **person** who has **many wives** is troubled when they try to attract him in their own way. Similalry, a **yogi** is also troubled when the **tongue** is attracted to palatable dishes; the **genitals** to sex, the **sense of touch** to contact with soft things; the **belly**, although filled, still wants to eat more; the **ear** attracted to cinema songs and so on. (7.9.40)

The Supreme Lord's Protection

26. Just as a **patient dies** in spite of a good **physician** and good **medicine**, similarly if the Supreme Lord does not give one protection, **one** must **suffer** in spite of the presence of his **father** and **mother**. (7.2.55 P)
27. Just as a **father** and **mother** cannot protect their **child**, a **physician** and **medicine** cannot relieve a **suffering patient**, a **boat** on the ocean cannot protect a **drowning man**, similarly those not cared by Lord cannot do anything for their betterment. (7.9.19)

The Demigods

28. One has to follow the laws made by the **government**, not by the **officers**. Similarly, everyone has to worship to the **Supreme Lord** only, not the **demigods**. (7.3.24 P)
29. If a dog is swimming in the water and one wants to cross the ocean by **catching hold of the dog's tail**, certainly he is foolish. Similarly, in distress if one **seeks shelter of a demigod**, he is foolish. (7.4.21 P)

About The Devotees

30. Just as the **moon** never refuses to distribute its pleasing rays even to the home of a *caṇḍāla*, similarly a **devotee** never refuses to act for everyone's welfare. (7.4.31-32 P)
31. Everything appears **yellow** to the **jaundiced eye**. Similarly, to a **pure devotee**, everyone appears to be engaged in **Kṛṣṇa's service**. (7.4.37 P)
32. Just as a **materialistic person** is always absorbed in thoughts of **material gain**, similarly a **pure devotee** is always absorbed in thoughts of **Kṛṣṇa**. (7.4.37 P)
33. A **cow** that is cared for by her master is not in anxiety over its maintenance and always **devoted to its master**, only for the **master's benefit**. Similarly, **one** who has no motive other than to **serve the Lord** surrenders everything to the Lord and acts only to **please Him**. (7.5.23-24 P)
34. An **expert geologist** can understand where there is **gold** and by various processes can extract it from the **gold ore**. Similarly, a **spiritually advanced person** can also understand how the **spiritual particle** exists within the **body**, and thus by cultivating spiritual knowledge he can attain perfection in spiritual life. (7.7.21)
35. An **iron rod** put into a **fire** becomes like fire. Similarly, when a **devotee** constantly engages in **bhakti**, he no longer has any material activities, for his body is spiritualized. (7.7.36 P)
36. Just as those who are **greedy** see everything as a source of **money-making** and those who are **lusty** see everything as being conducive to **sex**, similarly the **most perfect devotee**, Prahlāda saw **Nārāyaṇa** even within a stone column. (7.7.55 P)
37. **Lion** is very fearsome for **other animals**, but its **cubs** are not at all afraid of the lion. The **water of the sea** is certainly dreadful for all **living entities on the land**, but within the sea even the **small fish** is unafraid. Similarly, the **Lord** sometimes assumes a fierce appearance to kill the **demons**, but the **devotees** take pleasure in worshipping and glorifying the Lord in any form, either pleasing or fierce. (7.9.15 P)
38. If one's **face is decorated**, the **reflection** of one's face in a mirror is also seen to be decorated. Similarly, when **something is offered to Lord**, it is for the benefit of the

devotee, for the Lord does not need service from anyone. (7.9.11)

39. Just as a **person** inherits his **father's property**, a Kṛṣṇa conscious **devotee**, undisturbed by dualities, is sure to return **back to Godhead**. (7.9.31 P)
40. Just as a **wise man**, by considering cause and effect, can see how **fire pervades wood**, similarly **those** engaged in devotional service understand how the **Lord** is both the cause and effect. (7.9.47)
41. For a **person** who has **suitable shoes** on his feet, there is no **danger** even when he walks on pebbles and thorns. Similarly, for **one** who is always **self-satisfied** there is no **distress**; indeed, he feels happiness everywhere. (7.15.17)
42. If **someone** considers the **Supreme Lord** to be an ordinary human being, this does not mean He becomes ordinary. Similarly, if the **family members** of the **spiritual master** consider him as an ordinary human being, this does not mean that he becomes an ordinary. (7.15.27 P)

Material Desires and Attachments

43. **Blind men** guided by **another blind man** miss the right path and fall into a ditch. Similarly, **persons who are strongly entrapped** by material life, and who have accepted a **leader or guru** attached to external sense objects, cannot understand the goal of life. (7.5.31)
44. If one continuously sprinkles drops of ghee on a fire, the fire will not be extinguished, but if one suddenly puts a **lump of ghee on a fire**, the fire may possibly be **extinguished** entirely. Similarly, those who are too sinful are allowed to **enjoy sinful activities fully**, for thus there is a chance that these activities will become **detestful** to them, and they will get the opportunity to be purified. (7.11.33-34)
45. Just like a **silkworm**, which weaves a cocoon in which it becomes **imprisoned**, similarly the **attached householder** simply for the satisfaction of his genitals and tongue is **bound** by material conditions. (7.6.11-13)

Bhakti

46. When **one takes up spiritual activities**, one's entire **material body** is spiritualized. Similarly, in this material world, when **Kṛṣṇa consciousness expands**, the entire **material world** becomes spiritualized. (7.9.33 P
47. The idea that the **rope** is a **snake** is false, but the snake is not false. Similarly this **world**, which is full of varieties, is not false; it is a reflection of the reality in the **spiritual world**. (7.15.58 P)

General Wisdom

48. Although a **medicinal herb** does not belong to the same category as a man, if beneficial it is **kept very carefully**. Similarly, if **someone outside one's family** is favorable, he should be **given protection** like a son. On the other hand, if a **limb of one's body is poisoned** by disease, it must be **amputated** so that the rest of the body may live happily. Similarly, even one's **own son, if unfavorable**, must be **rejected**, although born of one's own body. (7.5.37)
49. Just as it is dangerous to **feed milk** to a **snake**, similarly it is dangerous to give benedictions to **demons**, who are by nature ferocious and jealous. (7.10.30)
50. If a **tiger** kills a man this is not sinful, but if a man kills another man this is considered sinful, and the killer is hanged. Similarly, the **men of the lower classes**, are accustomed to stealing, drinking and illicit sex, but that is not considered sinful. (7.10.31)
51. A **python**, although lying in one place, not endeavoring for its livelihood, gets the food it needs to **maintain body and soul**. Similarly, if a man is poor, he should not endeavor to improve his economic condition because **one who is desireless** also obtains his **livelihood** without endeavor. (7.15.15)
52. Just as **professional activities** or **business profits** cannot help one in spiritual advancement but are a source of material entanglement, so, the **Vedic ritualistic ceremonies** cannot help anyone who is not a devotee of the Supreme Lord. (7.15.29)
53. In general warfare one must take help from his **chariot** and **horses** in order to **conquer** his **enemy**, and after that he may give up the chariot and its paraphernalia. Similarly, as long as one has a **human body**, one should fully use it **to obtain** the **highest perfection of life**, namely going back to Godhead. (7.15.45 P)

About the Author

Gauranga Darshan Das, a disciple of His Holiness Radhanath Swami, is the Associate Dean of Academics Affairs, of the Bhaktivedanta Vidyapitha Research Center (BVRC)[11] at ISKCON Govardhan Eco Village (GEV). He holds a Masters degree from the Indian Institute of Science, Bangalore.

He teaches Srimad Bhagavatam, Sri Caitanya Caritamrita and Vaishnava Character courses at the Vidyapitha. He also travels to several places in India conducting scriptural courses.

Gauranga Darshan Das has written study guides including *Gītā Subodhinī*, *Bhāgavata Subodhinī* and *Caitanya Subodhinī* presenting the flow, context and gist of the scriptural contents in a simplified manner.

He has a special fondness for reciting and meditating on scriptural verses and has compiled vital verses in the form of books namely *Gītā Ratnamālā*, *Bhāgavata Ratnamālā*, *Caitanya Ratnamālā* and *Bhāgavata Tattvamāla*.

He also runs a free monthly e-magazine called *Bhāgavata Pradīpikā* and regularly writes educational and devotional articles that appear in the BTG International as well.

He is known for his spiritual discourses with captivating visuals and also presentations that give a birds' eye view of an entire book or a section. He has guided the students of several Vidyapitha batches, especially in their scriptural studies. He also oversees the Deity worship at GEV.

[11] www.vidyapitha.in, www.brcmumbai.com

Books By The Author

STUDY GUIDES

Gītā Subodhinī

Bhāgavata Subodhinī Cantos 1-2

Bhāgavata Subodhinī Canto 3

Bhāgavata Subodhinī Canto 4

Bhāgavata Subodhinī Cantos 5-6

Bhāgavata Subodhinī Cantos 7

Caitanya Subodhinī Ādi-līlā

Caitanya Subodhinī Madhya-līlā – I

Caitanya Subodhinī Madhya-līlā – II

Caitanya Subodhinī Antya-līlā

SLOKA BOOKS

(Pocket Size)

Gītā Ratnamālā

Bhāgavata Ratnamālā Cantos 1-6

Bhāgavata Ratnamālā Cantos 7-12

Caitanya Ratnamālā

Bhāgavata Tattvamālā